The Mental Compulsions Workbook for OCD

CBT and Mindfulness Skills to Navigate Intrusive Thoughts and Mental Traps

Lauren K. M. Rosen, LMFT

New Harbinger Publications, Inc.

Publisher's Note

New Harbinger Publications is an employee-owned company.

New Harbinger Publications, Inc.
5720 Shattuck Avenue
Oakland, CA 94609
www.newharbinger.com

Cover design by Amy Daniel

Acquired by Jess O'Brien

Edited by Kandace Little

Library of Congress Cataloging-in-Publication Data on file

Printed in the United States of America

28 27 26

10 9 8 7 6 5 4 3 2 1 First Printing

"There is a misconception in the obsessive-compulsive disorder (OCD) world that you can always tell when someone is engaging in a compulsion. We know that this is not true because we cannot see the mental compulsions that people are displaying in response to their obsessions. And, while we still cannot read the minds of those with OCD, we have a better insight into how they work, thanks to this excellent workbook that Lauren Rosen has written. Thank you for advancing the field and opening our eyes, our ears, and our minds to acknowledging, assessing, and treating the mental compulsion side of OCD."

—**Patrick B. McGrath, PhD**, chief clinical officer at NOCD, fellow of the Association for Behavioral and Contextual Science (ABCT), and author of *The OCD Answer Book* and *Don't Try Harder, Try Different*

"Lauren Rosen has written a clear, compassionate, and much-needed guide for tackling one of the most misunderstood aspects of OCD. This workbook is an essential tool for anyone struggling with mental rituals—and for clinicians supporting them."

—**Jonathan S. Abramowitz, PhD**, professor of psychology at the University of North Carolina at Chapel Hill, and author of *Getting Over OCD*

"In *The Mental Compulsions Workbook for OCD,* Lauren Rosen brings clarity to an issue that has long been a source of great confusion for OCD sufferers and treatment providers alike. When a person with OCD is engaged in mental activity that isn't working, what exactly are they doing in there? This warm and accessible workbook goes beyond simply naming mental compulsions and gives the reader concrete things to look for and do. Finally, a guide that offers more for addressing mental compulsions than 'Oh, just drop it.'"

—**Jon Hershfield, MFT**, director of The Center for OCD and Anxiety at Sheppard Pratt, author of *When a Family Member Has OCD*, and coauthor of *The Mindfulness Workbook for OCD*

"Mental compulsions are widely misunderstood, and as a result, often missed in the recovery from OCD. Lauren's book is an important step in working effectively with these peskier compulsions. Lauren is a compassionate person and therapist whose deep understanding of mindfulness as an antidote to mental compulsions is an asset to her patients, and her readers."

—**Stuart Ralph, MA, MSc**, creator of the *The OCD Stories* podcast, and cofounder of The Integrative Centre for OCD

For too long, mental compulsions have been overlooked in conversations about the OCD experience. Lauren Rosen's book fills this important gap with clarity and depth, offering innovative metaphors, relatable examples, and thoughtfully designed experiential exercises. Grounded in research yet written in compassionate, accessible language, it translates evidence-based principles into tools that both clinicians and individuals with OCD will find invaluable. This is a timely and much-needed contribution to the field."

—**Amy Mariaskin, PhD**, director of the Nashville OCD & Anxiety Treatment Center, and author of *Thriving in Relationships When You Have OCD*

"*The Mental Compulsions Workbook for OCD* is a master class in understanding mental rituals—the hidden villain of OCD. Lauren guides readers to disentangle obsessions from invisible compulsions, to accept intrusive thoughts and urges without judgment, and to reduce how frequently they get trapped in the vortex of OCD's endless mental loops. Grounded in evidence-based practices, this workbook transforms recovery into an empowering road map—from uncertainty to clarity; from compulsions to a life of intentionality and joy."

> —**Josh Spitalnick, PhD, ABPP**, owner and CEO of Anxiety Specialists of Atlanta, coauthor of *The Complete Guide to Overcoming Health Anxiety*, and codeveloper of the resource www.overcominghealthanxiety.com

"Mental compulsions may be the most confusing concept in the OCD and anxiety context. Lauren has done an amazing job addressing the most common sticking points. She addresses the topic in clear, easy-to-understand language. I found myself making notes while reading because I can use Lauren's explanations with my OCD therapy clients!"

> —**Drew Linsalata, MA, MHC-LP,** therapist; and host of the podcasts, *The Anxious Truth* and *Disordered*

"*The Mental Compulsions Workbook for OCD* is an essential read for anyone who has struggled to manage OCD's mental chatter. Lauren Rosen presents a trove of practical strategies in a relatable, compassionate, easy-to-read way that will give readers all the tools they need to feel more confident and effective in wrangling their busy minds."

> —**Ben Eckstein, LCSW**, owner and director of Bull City Anxiety & OCD Treatment Center, and author of *Worrying Is Optional*

"I'm impressed by *The Mental Compulsions Workbook for OCD*. As a clinician, I've used many workbooks in my practice, but this one shines above the rest. It's comprehensive, including action items, exercises, and interventions. As someone familiar with Lauren's work, I'm not surprised that this book is well written and researched. It includes up-to-date, evidence-based tools to overcome mental compulsions from a leader in the field who also lives with OCD. I'm excited to recommend this to clients!"

> —**Chris Trondsen, LMFT**, member of the International OCD Foundation (IOCDF)'s board of directors; and vice president of OCD Southern California, an official affiliate of the IOCDF

"*The Mental Compulsions Workbook for OCD* provides a clear and practical guide through a variety of approaches towards this often-hidden form of ritualizing. Using helpful diagrams and worksheets, readers will come away with a clearer understanding of what mental rituals are, and clear strategies for how best to slip out of their gravitational pull, to make room for discomfort and uncertainty, and into a freer and connected life."

> —**Lisa W. Coyne, PhD**, assistant professor in the department of psychiatry at Harvard Medical School/McLean, and CEO of the New England Center for OCD and Anxiety

To my darling dad who taught me that who dares wins.

To my sweetest mamacita who held me as I practiced daring and showed me how to hold myself.

To my remarkable husband who champions my daring and walks steadfastly beside me through it all.

And to my children who continually inspire me as they show me what it means to dare greatly.

May you, dear reader, dare to live your life on your terms in the face of discomfort and fear.

Contents

Foreword

When I was nine years old, I would sit by the window in our lounge room and stare out at the long concrete driveway that led up to our home and think,

My aunt will get into a car crash and die.

My aunt will get into a car crash and die.

I thought it not because I wanted it to happen, but so it wouldn't happen.

It didn't make logical sense—but I was not going to take any risks with the people I love. Even as a child, I knew that my thoughts weren't magical. But what if they were? What if the very act of not thinking something meant I wasn't doing my part to keep the people I loved safe?

Like so many people with OCD, I took the burden on myself and believed that by imagining the worst-case scenario, I could somehow prevent it. If I thought the unthinkable, I might be protecting my family.

No one knew. And that's often the case for people with intrusive thoughts. My guess is that you, too, may have suffered silently, terrified to speak your thoughts aloud. You probably fear that your thoughts might come true. Even worse, you likely fear the harsh judgments and reactions to your secret inner world. So, you try to reconcile your fears in your mind. These mental gymnastics take over every corner of our mind—controlling us, berating us, and taking away the things we value most: our joy, our relationships, our time.

Years later, I would learn these behaviors had a name: mental compulsions. And I would come to understand that I was far from alone.

In fact, millions of people with OCD engage in hours—sometimes entire days—of exhausting, invisible mental rituals. We do it to feel safe, to gain control, and most of all, to relieve or "solve" what feels like intolerable discomfort, anxiety, doubt, and uncertainty.

Three decades later, I've had the privilege of sitting across from hundreds of clients navigating that same storm. I've worked with people experiencing the most painful, unwanted, and terrifying thoughts—unimaginable thoughts that bring them to their knees, and make them cry, isolate, and question who they are. These are not just a few "bad thoughts." These are thoughts that make people believe they are broken and doubt whether they are even worthy of being here.

If you're holding this workbook, this story likely feels familiar because you, too, have tried everything to feel safe from your thoughts.

You're here because you want to reclaim your life from the grip of mental compulsions. And based on research, many people spend years—sometimes decades—trying to "solve" their way out of anxiety. Mental compulsions are often overlooked, even by well-trained clinicians. While physical compulsions are easier to spot, mental rituals like mental reassurance, mental review, mental rehearsal, or thought neutralization (just to name a few) can be just as debilitating, if not more so. And because many people don't even realize they're engaging in mental compulsions, they're often harder to identify.

That's where *The Mental Compulsion Workbook* comes in.

Lauren has crafted a compassionate, science-based guide that shines a light on the terrifying experience of intrusive thoughts, feelings, sensations, urges, and images—and the mental compulsions we use to try to find relief. She offers a clear, practical, and evidence-based path forward. She walks you through the inner workings of OCD and helps you understand why resisting the urge to do mental compulsions can seem so impossible—and yet, why it's one of the most empowering things you can learn to do.

My hope is that as you turn these pages, you'll not only discover how to interrupt your mental rituals but also how to treat yourself with fierce compassion every single step of the way. In your hands, you hold a distinct guide to help you break the cycle of obsessions and compulsions. By the end, you'll understand yourself and your condition more deeply. And you'll learn to stand tall, even as you lean into discomfort.

As an OCD specialist, I've seen the strategies and tools outlined in this book change the lives of so many—people stepping back into their lives, freer, more confident, and no longer ruled by fear. With Lauren's extensive experience and wise words, all backed by research and science, you too can go on to live your most beautiful life.

So before we part and you dive into the good stuff, let's make a deal:

As you move forward, gift yourself as much kindness and compassion as you can. And bravely commit to making you the priority as you navigate this work.

You are not your thoughts.

You are not your compulsions.

You are someone learning to live—braveheartedly—even when fear shows up.

With love and deep respect,

—Kimberley Quinlan, LMFT

Introduction

Fourteen to seventeen years?! How could it take fourteen to seventeen years on average for a person with obsessive compulsive disorder to get a correct diagnosis and proper treatment?

I put down the article I was reading to digest the reality behind those numbers. Fourteen years until diagnosis means 5,110 days of struggling with an overwhelming sense of terror, 122,640 hours going toe to toe with an unnamed rival you don't know how to fight, or 7,358,400 minutes ruled by thoughts and emotions. This is the *average* experience someone with OCD has before getting a correct diagnosis (IOCDF 2014).

How can it take so long?

My ten years of experience as a psychotherapist specializing in the treatment of OCD has shown that one of the foremost factors behind delayed diagnosis is a lack of awareness about what OCD really looks like. The media reduces OCD to leaping over sidewalk cracks, locking doors, and washing hands. Because of this, people are mostly unaware that OCD can be invisible to the naked eye. Many professionals and most laypeople are completely unaware of mental compulsions.

Depending on the source you look at, the estimated prevalence of mental compulsions varies. Research suggests that most people with OCD perform mental compulsions (Shavitt et al. 2014). Some place specific estimates at 55.4 percent (Ferrão et al. 2023) while others place them at 53.7 percent (Pal et al. 2024). One study states that 12.9 percent of individuals with OCD *primarily* engage in mental compulsions (Sibrava et al. 2011). No matter how you slice it, many people with OCD struggle with mental compulsions, and getting proper help is nearly impossible when the vast majority of folks have no frame of reference for what's happening in their minds.

From the time I learned about the fourteen-to-seventeen-year statistic, I knew I wanted to be a part of changing it. It informed my choice to become a psychotherapist specializing in OCD. It ignited my passion for advocacy. It drove me to educate others about what OCD looks like and how it's treated. Ultimately, though, I don't believe my career or commitment to supporting others accounts for why that statistic stuck with me. I think its staying power was down to a single factor:

It was personal.

I didn't receive my OCD diagnosis until I was twenty-four years old, but, when I did, my therapist helped bring new clarity to my most challenging childhood memories. He also gave me that article—the one with the fourteen-to-seventeen year statistic. As I read those numbers it dawned on me: I had lived with the disorder for seventeen years. So, I remember those numbers because they validated almost two decades of deeply confusing and painful experiences.

I was fortunate to find a therapist who knew all about mental compulsions and saw what others had missed. With his help, I've built a life that is fulfilling and meaningful in a way that I never dreamed possible while in the throes of OCD. I got my life back, and I want to help you find the contentment I've found in recovery.

Who This Book Is For

If you struggle with obsessions but can't see any compulsive *behaviors,* this book is for you. If you want to get a better grasp of what mental compulsions are and how to deal with them, this book is for you. If you constantly find yourself stuck in your head, this book is for you. In it, I'll help you understand the mechanics of OCD and teach you how to effectively address your symptoms so you can get back to creating a life worth living.

I hope you didn't have to wait seventeen years. I hope you didn't have to wait one year. But no matter how long the wait, picking up this book and educating yourself puts you on the path to reclaiming your life. Based on my experience and the experiences of the many clients I've walked through this process, the principles in this book can help change your inner world. OCD makes life appear bleak and hopeless, but I can assure you, your world can transform in the most unexpected and beautiful ways.

How to Use This Workbook

The aim of this workbook is twofold. First, to help you understand the ins and outs of mental compulsions. To accomplish this we'll cover:

- what mental compulsions are
- what they are not
- why you perform them
- how they cause issues in your life
- how to identify them
- how to disengage from them

Establishing all of this is critical. If you don't understand what mental compulsions are and how they work, then you can't navigate them effectively. Ultimately, though, understanding is not enough. If you want your life to change, you'll have to let the ideas in this book guide your choices.

It's like driving a car. It's important to read about driving and take driver's ed, but this alone can't get you from point A to point B. You will have to get behind the wheel. Likewise, knowing how to spot and drop mental compulsions is different from actually interrupting them and reorienting your attention.

If you want these ideas to transform your day-to-day life and catapult you into recovery, I encourage you to take this book at a slow and steady pace so you can put its ideas to the test and establish practical skills. There's no need to rush! The answer to recovery isn't at the end of this book; rather, the path to recovery is in its pages.

While you're reading, stop to reflect on and respond to the journal prompts. These exercises are steps between understanding this book conceptually and putting its contents into practice. You can find downloadable versions of many of these exercises and audio resources online at http://www.newharbinger.com/55541. You may be tempted to read quickly through exercises because you find that the ideas are simple. Keep in mind, though, that simple doesn't mean easy. Putting these concepts into action is hard work and making use of the practices in this book can ease you into living out the concepts detailed in it.

Think of this more as an instructional guide than a book. Its contents will serve you best if you consult it regularly as you go about the task of living. Ultimately, recovery requires a paradigm shift that is counterintuitive for most of us. Reflecting on these concepts regularly can support you in approaching your experiences through the lens of recovery instead of reverting to the patterns that led you to pick up this book.

I recommend keeping a journal handy while working through this workbook and jotting down ideas that stand out to you. In my work, I've found that reading through such notes once daily helps people keep recovery concepts at the forefront of their minds and continually make use of what they're learning.

A Roadmap

We'll start by exploring the basics. We'll cover what mental compulsions are, different ways they might appear, and why it's important that we understand them. We'll discuss the differences between automatic thoughts, mental compulsions, emotions, and other internal experiences so that you can identify each and navigate them all more effectively. Once we've got this established, we'll talk about mental compulsions' role in perpetuating OCD and causing suffering.

After we have a clear understanding of what mental compulsions are and what OCD's playbook looks like, we can develop a game plan using cognitive behavioral therapy (CBT), exposure and response prevention (ERP), acceptance and commitment therapy (ACT), and mindfulness-based interventions.

Throughout the book, I'll use different manifestations of OCD to exemplify different concepts. Whether they directly relate to your experience of OCD or not, they should help you apply these principles to your experience. They may also, incidentally, be triggering at times. Such triggers are an unavoidable byproduct of pursuing a meaningful life. At the same time, this book is intended to support you in navigating triggers. Given this, I hope you don't let the potential for discomfort stop you from reading further and gathering tools to support yourself.

Applying the ideas outlined in this book can be challenging! If you find yourself struggling to implement the concepts, professional help can be a valuable resource. While this book—or any book, for that matter—isn't a substitute for therapy, you can certainly explore its contents with a therapist or use it as an adjunct to treatment.

I'm so glad that you've picked up this workbook and hope that it will help you understand the inner workings of the obsessive-compulsive mind. For those of us with OCD, this understanding is the foundation of freedom. This knowledge is the springboard from which we can take our lives back so we can live them wholly on our own terms. With that said, here's to your recovery journey!

Part I

Setting the Scene

Before we talk about how to support yourself, we'll first establish what's happening in that brain of yours. If you want to better operate your mind, you have to understand the machinery. These first three chapters will help you understand the landscape of your mind so you can navigate it more effectively.

Chapter 1

What Are Mental Compulsions?

Have you ever found yourself saying, "I can't stop obsessing"? It's a common complaint among those with OCD. I hear it, or something like it, all the time. It could sound like "I was obsessing all day!" or "I've been obsessing about this nonstop!"

Most people don't realize that the term "obsessing" usually refers to two different experiences:

1. Obsessions, the *thoughts* that pop into your mind, make you aware of uncertainty or cause discomfort, and

2. Mental compulsions, the *thinking* you do to resolve the uncertainty and discomfort that obsessions bring up.

So, part of "obsessing" involves experiencing obsessions. You might, for example, have a thought pop into your mind like *What if I am a bad person?* But the other half of the equation, trying to figure out if you're a bad person, isn't obsessing. It's a mental compulsion.

"Obsessing" Part One: Experiencing an Obsession

Obsessions can be about different topics and are as varied as the individuals who experience them. Imagine, for a moment, the following scenarios:

> You're walking away from your home when you have the thought: *What if I didn't lock my door and someone breaks in?*
>
> You're walking down the street when an image of your car colliding with another flashes in your mind. You think, *Did that actually happen?*
>
> You're in the middle of writing an email when you think, *What if I wrote something obscene?*

You're eating a salad and suddenly you become hyperaware of the crunching sound. You're troubled by your awareness. You wonder, *Will I ever be able to focus on anything else?*

These are all examples of obsessions.

Obsessions are distressing thoughts, images, and urges. They are repetitive. Like a boomerang, they always seem to find their way back to you. People often think of obsessions as sticky—kind of like gum that gets lodged on your shoe.

An obsession is a passive experience, not an active one. What do I mean by active and passive experiences? Well, getting hit by a baseball is a passive experience, while throwing a baseball is an active one.

Obsessions are automatic and outside of your control. You're going about your day when you're reminded of some uncertainty that scares you or have a thought that makes you uncomfortable. Bam! You got hit by a thought, just like you might get hit by a baseball! You'd rather not have this thought, just like you'd rather not take a baseball to your forehead. These experiences are unwanted.

Breaking Down Your Obsessions

Let's get to know your obsessions.

Do you ever say that you've been obsessing about something? This might sound like:

"I am obsessing over what decision to make."

"I'm obsessing about ______________________________."

- whether or not [something will happen]
- symmetry
- how gross that is
- the fact that I can see my nose

"I'm obsessing about whether or not I am ______________________________."

- a good person
- going to heaven/hell
- in the "right" relationship
- actually attracted to my partner
- attracted to a certain gender
- really alive

- mentally ill
- in denial about a memory being "real"
- going to suffer forever
- going to take my own life
- a murderer
- a sociopath
- attracted to an inappropriate age group

Jot down anything you obsess about or over.

Now that you've identified what you obsess over, we know what theme(s) your obsessions generally revolve around.

Let's turn our attention to the related doubtful or distressing thoughts, images, or urges within the theme(s): obsessions.

Individual obsessions within each theme can vary widely. For example, someone might struggle with the central concern "What if I'm in the 'wrong' relationship?" and experience different obsessions like:

"What if I am attracted to that person?"

"What if I have an affair?"

"What if I'm lying to myself?"

You may have started noticing that the words "what if" are repeated a lot. If you have OCD, you can view these words as a huge red flag. That's because obsessions often involve doubt. Indeed, an intolerance of uncertainty and anxiety is one of the most common threads of the obsessive-compulsive experience. That's why it's called the doubting disorder.

The "what if" may be explicit. For instance, you might recognize the words "What if I'm a murderer?" cross your mind. Even when the words "what if" aren't immediately evident in your thoughts, though, doubt is typically at the center of obsessions.

OCD sufferers find "what ifs," whether implied or explicit, to be highly distressing. That's because they highlight uncertainty, and people with OCD tend to be intolerant of doubt. Whether the thought is *What if I'm a bad person?* or *What if I'm living in a simulation?*, those with OCD don't want to accept even the slightest possibility that their thoughts might reflect reality.

What's Your "What If"?

"What ifs" aren't part of everyone's obsessions, but since they can be implicit, it's helpful to consider if your obsessions involve doubt.

Identifying what you obsess over can help you boil down your fears into a "what if." For instance, if you obsess over whether you're going to hell, then you're probably afraid of the possibility that you'll go to hell, and the corresponding "what if" would be "What if I'm going to hell?" If you obsess over whether you're actually alive, then you're probably afraid that you could be dead, and the corresponding "what if" would be "What if I'm already dead?"

Ultimately, what you "obsess over" is probably the possibility that you fear, and your "what if" will be "What if that possibility comes to pass?" If you've identified a "what if," note it in the space below.

____

____

____

____

____

____

____

If you can't come up with anything now, pay attention over the course of the next week then come back to jot down what you notice.

Whether explicit or implicit, "what if" thoughts can be triggered by many different experiences, both internal and external. A "what if" might occur after another automatic thought. Let's say you're spending time with a platonic friend when you think, *Kiss them!* This might lead you to wonder, *What if having that thought means I'm going to kiss them?* Both the command thought "Kiss them!" and the "what if" interpretation that follows would be considered obsessions.

So, obsessions can present as statements and command thoughts. They can also present as images. If you're hanging out with that friend and an explicit image of them pops into your head, this is an obsession, and so are the thoughts of concern that may follow, like:

Why would I imagine that? What if this means I'm in the wrong relationship?

or

What if I can't shake that thought and it ruins my evening?

Obsessions can also involve impulses or urges. You might notice the urge to make items symmetrical or to wash your hands to get rid of a feeling of discomfort or disgust. You might notice a surge of energy traveling toward your mouth as you pass by your friend and interpret this physical sensation as an urge to kiss them. This could lead you to fret, *Why would I have that urge? What does that mean about my relationship?* Here, both the surge of energy and the feared meaning of that energy are obsessions.

Ultimately, a book could be written about the ways obsessions can present. But that's not this book. For our purposes, the important thing is to help you map your experience and better navigate it. For most, intrusive images, command thoughts, and impulses will be accompanied by some interpretation. This interpretation will usually involve some doubt and can probably be boiled down to a "what if." Given this, we will talk a lot about "what ifs" and doubt in this book.

If you don't believe you are making meaning of the thoughts, images, and urges, it is possible that doubt isn't central in your experience of OCD. There may be a hidden "what if" in your experience—like the fear that if you don't do something, the obsessions or emotions could last forever. But you may simply want the experience—the image, for example—to go away because you don't want to feel discomfort. This tends to happen in iterations of OCD that center on disgust, hyperawareness, making things "just right," and achieving symmetry. If the urge to rid yourself of an experience drives your compulsions, and you can't parse any fears related to doubt, just know that the sections related to uncertainty may not apply in your situation.

Whether you're trying to get rid of thoughts pertaining to doubt, scary images, or even emotions like disgust, guilt, or discomfort, you are resisting unwanted experiences. Understanding your automatic experiences and the ways you resist them will help you address the factors that keep you stuck compulsing.

"Obsessing" Part Two: Performing Mental Compulsions

When people with OCD experience an obsession, they feel discomfort and want to do *something* to get relief from this discomfort. Enter part two of "obsessing": mental compulsions.

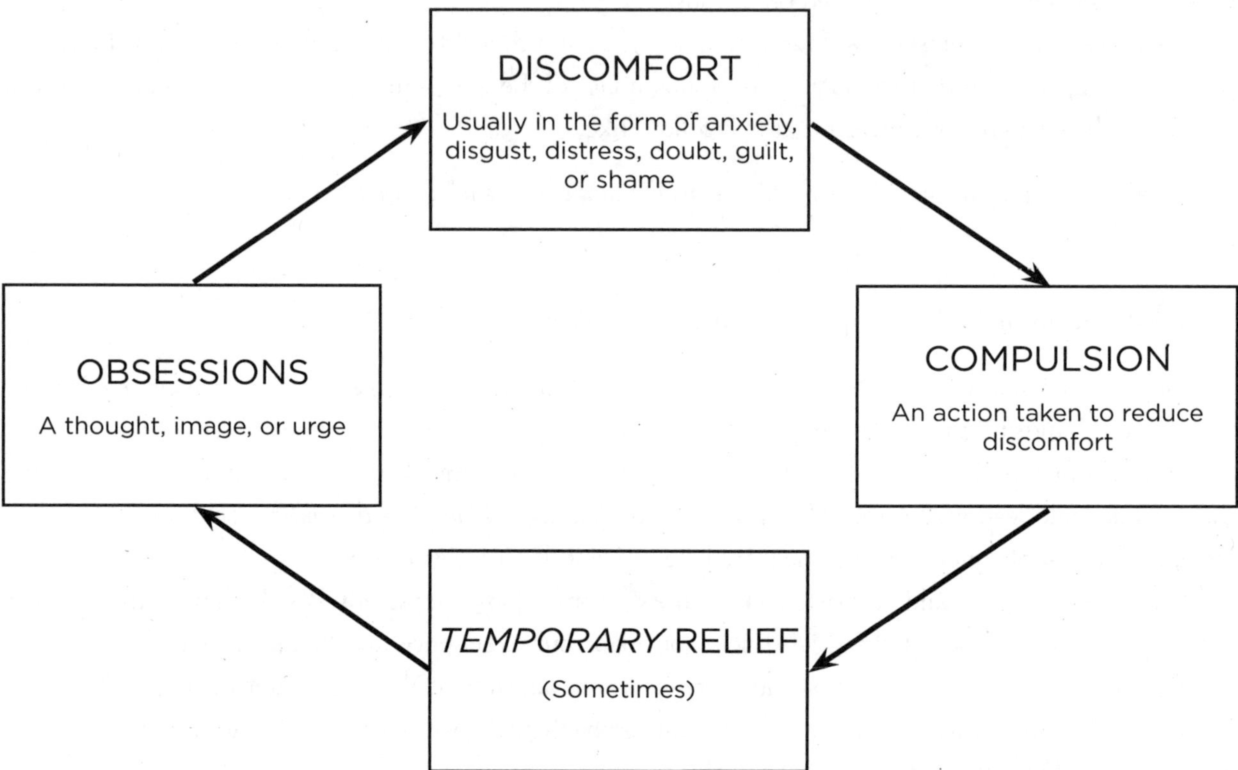

As you can see in the diagram, the obsession causes discomfort. If I have the thought *What if I'm a murderer?* I might experience any number of emotions like anxiety or guilt. This emotion is followed by a behavior that's intended to get rid of the feeling.

With mental compulsions, this behavioral response involves *active* thinking. For instance, when a person with OCD thinks, *What if I want to murder my family?*, they may

- worry about whether they have any intent to act on their thoughts
- debate whether they're capable of harming someone
- analyze their feelings toward family members
- review past interactions to determine if they have shown signs of violence

These attempts to figure out "whether I want to murder my family" are mental *compulsions*. If we return to the baseball analogy, we're no longer talking about getting hit. Mental compulsions involve running after the baseball that's hit you, picking it up, and tossing it around. This is an active process rather than a passive experience.

This idea that thinking is a compulsion may seem confusing. The term compulsion probably calls to mind images of people checking locks or washing excessively. And, yes, these are ways in which people perform compulsions. But compulsions can also be invisible. Sometimes they are all in our minds.

Even though they occur internally, mental compulsions are just like their visible counterparts in most respects. As with handwashing or door-checking, active thinking is a *behavior*. And just as people with OCD wash their hands to resolve uncertainty and discomfort, they also try to *think* their way out of uncertainty and discomfort.

For the most part, people with OCD do compulsions, mental or otherwise, to get rid of distress that results from obsessions. When this distress involves doubt, mental compulsions aim to address uncertainty about potential dreaded outcomes, no matter how unlikely these outcomes may be. When the distress involves other forms of discomfort, mental compulsions attempt to resolve that discomfort.

Your Mental Compulsions

Now that we've isolated your obsessions, take a moment to consider how you try to resolve whatever distress, doubt, or anxiety they cause. Are you responding to a demand like *I must pray five times or else something bad will happen*? Are you reviewing past experiences to get an answer? Are you trying to push your thoughts out of your mind? Describe how you try to resolve the uncomfortable emotions that obsessions create:

____

____

____

____

____

____

____

____

Exploring Common Mental Compulsions

Given that mental compulsions can't be seen, labeling some common ones can help us to better recognize them.

While obsessions create discomfort or call something into question, the compulsion involves attempts to figure things out, neutralize threats, or get rid of emotions.

How do you try to neutralize or "figure things out?" Do you:

- Analyze thoughts?
- Argue with thoughts?
- Try to predict and resolve potential risks?
- Wish thoughts away?
- Review a past event or rehearse for a potential future?
- Repeat phrases to yourself to prevent catastrophe?
- Beat yourself up for having thoughts?

Review these mental compulsions and consider whether any match your experience:

Mental Reassurance: Reassuring yourself excessively that something is or will be okay. For example: "I would never hurt my child. That's just not me."

Mental Review: Reviewing conversations or experiences to get certainty about what happened.

Mental Rehearsal: Replaying possible outcomes in your head to prevent or "problem-solve" some dreaded outcome. Note: this is different from planning, which is time-limited and action-oriented. Mental rehearsal involves excessive attempts to plan when an outcome is unlikely or planning isn't possible.

Mental Checking: Recalling a prior check to ensure the check was thorough.

Compulsive Prayer: Repeating a prayer to (a) make sure that something bad doesn't occur or (b) neutralize a "bad" thought or feeling.

Rumination: Excessively reviewing the same information with the intent of extracting meaning, determining relevance, or predicting consequences. The review usually concerns past events and is philosophical in nature. The term also refers to ruminants, a class of animals who chew food, swallow it, regurgitate it, and chew it more. When it comes to mental rumination, people "chew" on a concern and "let it digest" (i.e., commit to leaving it alone) only briefly before "regurgitating" the content to "chew on" (reassess, reconsider) it more. Many use rumination as a catchall to refer to excessive thinking.

Excessive Analysis: Reviewing the same information repeatedly, investigating finer details, and picking apart evidence to get to the bottom of a question.

Mental Debate: Arguing with yourself to figure out what's "right" or "true."

Worry: Worry, like rumination, involves repeatedly considering information, though worry usually refers to concerns about future events. While worry can refer to an emotional experience, the mental compulsion involves the act of mulling over information.

Self-Flagellation: Mentally beating yourself up to atone for perceived misdeeds.

Scenario Bending: Considering the various ways a scenario could have played out, often to check how you would feel or behave in hypothetical situations.

Thought Neutralizing: Thinking a "good" thought to counteract a "bad" one.

Counting: Counting to a "good" number, often to neutralize a "bad" thought, set things "right," or prevent catastrophe.

Memory Hoarding: Trying to hold on to every aspect of a memory in perfect detail.

Thought Suppression: Attempting to push thoughts out of awareness.

Emotional Checking: Checking your emotional temperature to ensure that your feelings are aligned with what you deem appropriate.

Mental Tracking: Keeping track of what has directly or indirectly come into contact with contaminants.

Mental Tracing: Drawing pictures or symbols in your mind's eye or moving your eyes in a ritualized pattern.

Mental Repetition: Repeating a phrase a certain number of times or until it feels "just right" to avoid catastrophe or sidestep discomfort.

Checking Sensations: Scanning your body for physical sensations to ensure that you are having what you deem to be appropriate physical sensations in the given circumstances.

Replaying: Playing scenes, whether real or imagined, repeatedly in your mind.

While most people engage in some of these mental behaviors, their frequency and function vary between individuals and mental health challenges. When looking at this list, what mental compulsions do you perform in response to your obsessions? Describe one mental compulsion you perform that fits these categories.

____

____

____

____

Labeling mental compulsions can help you to better identify and address them, but it's not important to perfectly pinpoint the "right" category. Your mental compulsions might not fit neatly into any of these labels. You may engage in several simultaneously; for example, reviewing a memory to check your emotions. Remember: these categories are meant to help you explore your mental compulsions and to support your awareness.

Labeling Unique Mental Compulsions

If you can't locate your brand of mental compulsions above, don't worry! This list isn't exhaustive. Let's label your mental compulsion(s). Reflect on the journaling you did in the prompt titled "Your Mental Compulsions." Now, boil down any behavior you described, as though you were trying to explain it to someone else. For instance, if you find yourself moving objects in your mind's eye so that you don't need to physically move the object, you might call this "mental moving" or "mental ordering." Label any unique mental compulsions on the provided lines:

____

____

____

____

The Difference Between Obsessions and Mental Compulsions

Given that obsessions and mental compulsions are both happening in your mind, it can be difficult to parse them. But as we've been discussing, there are key differences between obsessions, which are automatic thoughts, images, and urges, and mental compulsions, which are behaviors that involve active mental processes. Let's break them down.

Passive Thoughts vs. Active Thinking

Obsessions involve *passive* thoughts and compulsions involve *active* thinking. To illustrate the differences, let's take a brief detour into the wonderful world of math. (I promise this won't hurt *too* much.)

Chances are that 1+1= elicits an automatic response. When you read that equation, the number 2 likely occurred to you without much effort on your part. Likewise, obsessions are automatic, *passive* experiences.

I'm willing to bet that reading 5,478 x 264 doesn't bring an immediate answer to mind. For most people, this more complex multiplication requires intentional calculation or *active* thinking. Like this second math problem, mental compulsions require effort. Because of this, they can also be interrupted and dropped.

Problems vs. Solutions

Let's consider the difference between an obsession and a compulsion by considering their function. We can usually divvy obsessions and compulsions into problems and attempted solutions. Obsessions introduce a problem—something you don't like—and compulsions aim to address this problem. We ruminate, review, rehearse, pray, or somehow mentally compulse to solve the issue the obsession introduced.

Obsessions (Questions)	Compulsions (Seeking answers)
An image of a ___________ pops into your head	Thinknig a "good thought to neutralize the bad one

Since obsessions often generate doubt, the problem-solution pairing often occurs as a question (obsession) and seeking answers (compulsion).

Obsessions (Questions)	Compulsions (Seeking answers)
What if I will be damned to hell because I didn't give money to that person on the freeway offramp?	Mentally reviewing quotes from scripture to prove that you are not "bad."
What if hitting my brakes leads other cars to brake, indirectly causing a fatal collision?	Reviewing a memory of what you saw in the rearview mirror after hitting your brakes to "prove" that your action did not cause someone's death.

All this to say, if a distress-inducing or doubt-provoking question pops up, that's likely an obsession, but if you start trying to answer that question, you've likely wandered into compulsive territory.

Before we move on, take a moment to consider the problems or questions you experience and how you attempt to resolve them. Look at the examples on the previous page and then fill in your own. You can also find a copy of this chart at http://www.newharbinger.com/55541.

Obsessions (Questions)	Compulsions (Seeking answers)

What Is the Purpose of Your Mental Compulsions?

Revisit your list of mental compulsions and consider what you're *hoping* to get out of doing these compulsions. Please note—this is not the same as what you *actually get* out of these compulsions. What you're hoping to get and what the behavior actually accomplishes are often very different.

Consider these examples:

If you have sexual orientation OCD, and you analyze feelings in your groin, what are you hoping the analysis will prove? For many with this theme, the aim is to ensure that their attraction is consistent with their identified sexual orientation. They hope that proving this can eliminate anxiety related to the idea of being inauthentic.

If you have existential OCD and you're worried that you're living in a simulation, you might check your emotional experience to see if you "feel real." The goal here might be to prove that you're not living in a simulation so that you can get rid of the distress you feel about this idea.

What are your goals when performing mental compulsions?

____

____

____

____

____

____

____

____

So, to briefly review:

Obsessions:

- Are intrusive thoughts, images, and urges that often include "what if" thoughts
- Are automatic, passive experiences
- Pose problems or questions
- Cause anxiety, doubt, distress, guilt, shame, discomfort, disgust

Mental Compulsions

- Are mental behaviors
- Are habitual though not automatic
- Involve an active process
- Attempt to resolve or answer problems or questions

- Intend to resolve emotions that obsessions generate

Now that you have a better sense of the differences between obsessions and mental compulsions, let's explore how obsessions and mental compulsions play out in different OCD subtypes.

Chapter 2

Mental Compulsions Across Subtypes

Now that we understand what obsessions and mental compulsions are, let's consider how they often show up with OCD. The operative word here is "often." This list isn't exhaustive. It's intended to help you recognize your own obsessions and compulsions while giving us a framework for discussing mental compulsions throughout this book.

OCD Subtypes

OCD is often broken down into subtypes—like the themes people "obsess over" that we discussed in chapter 1. Let's explore some common subtypes and examples of obsessions within these themes:

Scrupulosity OCD:

- intrusive, immoral, or sacrilegious images
- upsetting command thoughts related to immoral or sacrilegious acts
- concerns like *What if I'm not moral or faithful enough?*

Real Event OCD:

- images or memories of an event
- concerns like *What if I am a monster because of something I did?*

Relationship OCD:

- unwanted urges to break up
- thoughts like *What if I'm in the wrong relationship?*

Sexual Orientation OCD:

- upsetting command thoughts like *Kiss them!*
- intrusive images of sexual acts
- concerns like *What if I'm not identifying as my authentic self?*

Existential OCD:

- feeling "unreal"
- concerns like *What if my reality is not as I believe it to be?*

Mental Health OCD:

- thoughts like *What if I have psychosis?*

False Memory OCD:

- mental images of a possible event
- concerns like *What if that mental image is a memory?*

Hyper-Awareness Obsessions:

- repetitive thoughts and images
- thoughts like *What if I never stop thinking about my breath?*

Self-Harm OCD:

- intrusive images of self-harm
- thoughts like *What if I want to kill myself?*

Harm OCD:

- intrusive violent images
- concerns like *What if I want to harm someone?*

Pedophilia-Themed OCD:

- upsetting, graphic images
- thoughts like *What if I want to harm a child?*

Contamination OCD:

- images of triggering substances
- thoughts like *What if I get sick because I touched that and infect an immunocompromised person?*

Just Right OCD:

- the urge to adjust something until it feels just right

Recovery-Related Obsessions:

- concerns like *What if my obsessions ruin my life?*

For many, OCD will jump from one theme to another. For others, it will stick relentlessly to one topic. Some experience multiple subtypes at the same time. For example, one person could have obsessions about harming others (harm OCD) *and* other obsessions about being in the wrong relationship (relationship OCD). Some people's obsessions combine several themes. You might have intrusive thoughts of self-harm (self-harm OCD) and worry that you will go to hell for having these thoughts (religious scrupulosity). Here is a Venn diagram to illustrate:

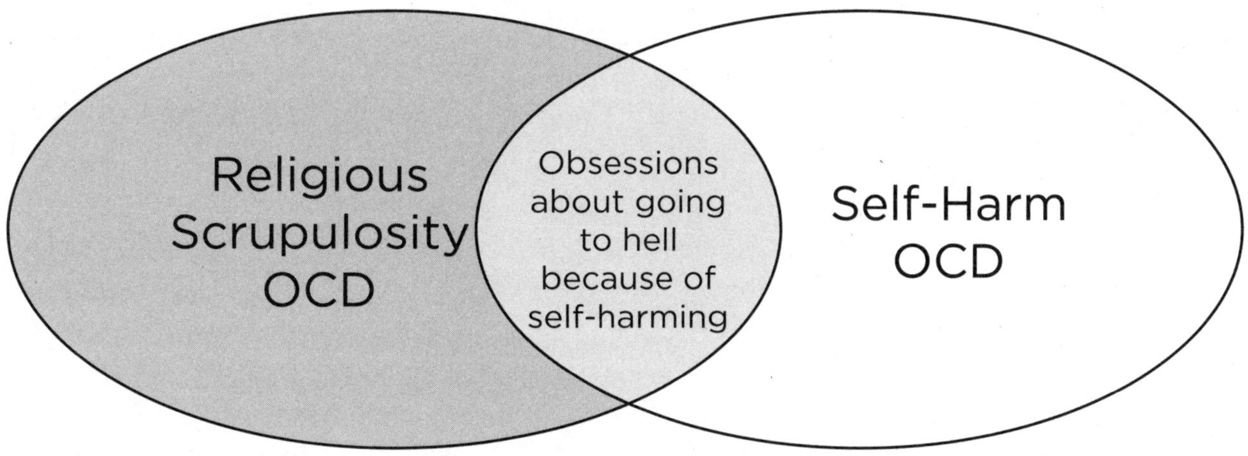

Ultimately, if we could draw a massive Venn diagram of subtypes, most, if not all, of the circles would intersect with other circles. It's difficult and ultimately unimportant to determine where one category begins and the next one ends.

Do you recognize your experience in these subtypes?

____

____

Do you have obsessions related to different subtypes? Have your obsessions changed over time?

____

____

____

____

Overlapping Subtypes

Are your obsessions a blend of different subtypes? Use the space below to draw your own Venn diagram.

Your obsessions might not fit into any of these categories or be represented in the examples I've listed. If your obsessions don't fit into any of the subtypes above, what would you call your own subtype?

___

___

Whether or not you recognize the *content* of your thoughts in the examples outlined above, the recovery *process* is, by and large, the same. That's because the process of OCD doesn't change from theme to theme.

The content of your obsessions is whatever topic scares you. With relationship-related obsessions, the content is likely about the quality of your relationship or partner. Meanwhile, with harm-related obsessions, the content of your thoughts is likely related to harm.

Reflect on the content of your thoughts. What ideas cause you distress?

___

___

___

___

While the content can vary widely, the process in OCD is universal: across the various subtypes, the content of obsessions is followed by attempts to resolve associated doubt and discomfort. People with relationship OCD feel discomfort related to doubt about the quality of their relationship and attempt to resolve this distress. Likewise, people with harm OCD experience discomfort related to images or doubt about what images mean and try to resolve their distress. In both cases, there is distress and then compulsions intended to resolve that discomfort.

Can you identify the process of resolving doubt or discomfort in your own experience?

___

___

___

When people start down the road to recovery, they usually think their theme is one of the worst, if not the worst. Many wish they had some other obsession, even one that's troubled them historically. It's the fact that the content matters to each individual that gives obsessions their emotional charge and keeps people stuck in the process of performing compulsions.

Even so, the process is what matters when it comes to diagnosing OCD. We diagnose obsessive-compulsive disorder, not existential OCD, harm OCD, and the like. And, by and large, because themes *function* in the same way, the content of the OCD doesn't change the path to recovery.

Now let's review the pattern of OCD that we discussed in chapter 1 so we can better understand how the process plays out with the different themes. Bear in mind that this is intentionally simplified to help you see how the cycle operates for you. In practice, the path from obsessions to compulsions may not always be so linear or even begin with an obsession.

The Obsessive-Compulsive Cycle

The cycle starts when an obsession pops into your mind, causing you discomfort. You want to get rid of this discomfort, so you do a compulsion to get rid of the feeling.

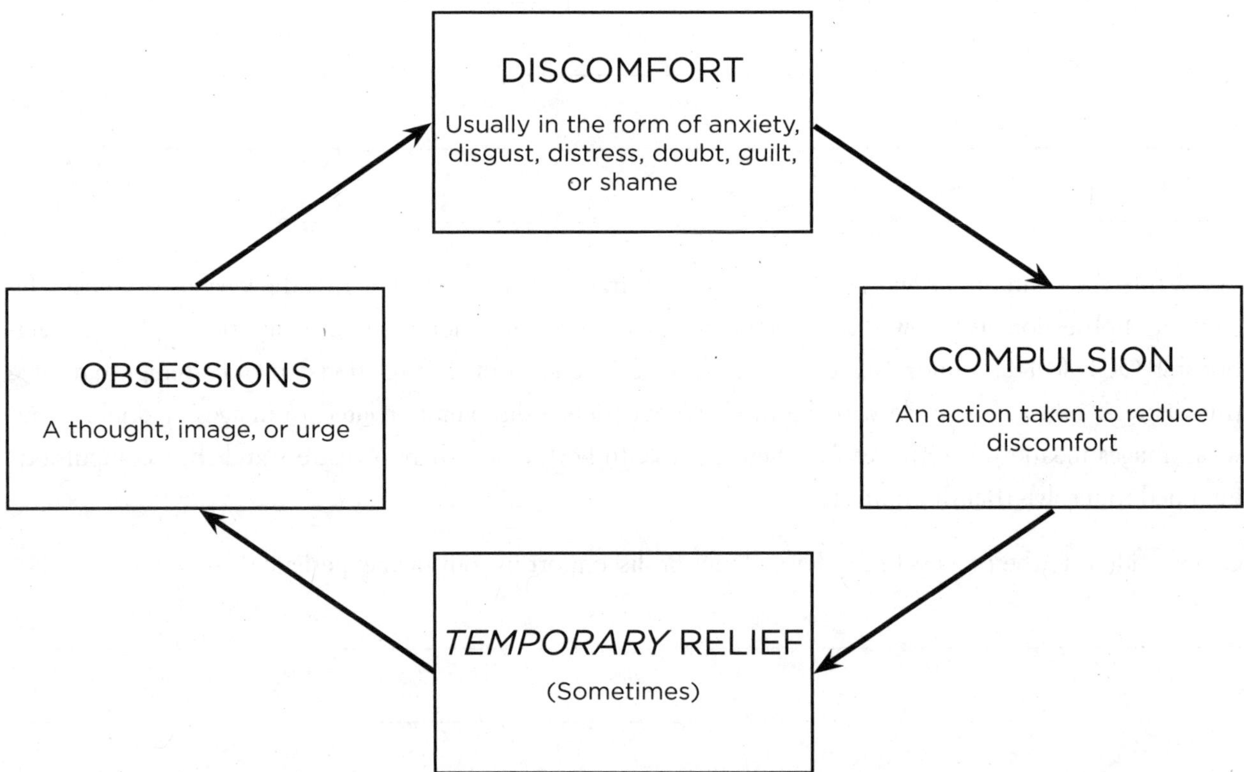

Sometimes compulsions get rid of feelings, but uncomfortable emotions and uncertainty cannot be completely and permanently resolved. When the thoughts and feelings inevitably resurface, people will repeat compulsions because they once led to relief.

But just as the effects of alcohol use eventually create more distress for someone experiencing addiction, the effects of compulsions ultimately create more distress for the OCD sufferer. Someone experiencing addiction might drink to forget about a fight with a friend, only to get into another drunken brawl. Likewise, someone with real event OCD might try to resolve doubt by mentally reviewing a situation, only to recognize more uncertainty that retriggers anxiety. Unfortunately, all it takes is some "successful" compulsions to hook the person with OCD and make them slaves to compulsions.

Why Do Subtypes Matter?

If the subtypes don't address everyone's experiences and don't substantially change our approach to recovery, you might wonder why these subtypes exist and why I've devoted a chapter to discussing them.

First, the subtypes increase awareness of OCD's many manifestations. A few one-dimensional portrayals of OCD dominate popular culture, so most people's experiences aren't represented. This can prevent individuals from recognizing symptoms as markers of OCD and stop people from getting help.

Additionally, exploring common themes can help you apply the concepts discussed in this book. While the overall goal is to better navigate distress and doubt, understanding how the intolerance of distress and doubt shows up in different subtypes helps with applying therapeutic concepts effectively.

In addition, different beliefs are common to different subtypes. People with harm OCD often believe thoughts are as bad as behaviors—a concept known as thought-action fusion. People with relationship OCD often have all-or-none views about what relationships should look like. Addressing these subtype-specific nuances can support recovery.

Exploring OCD Subtypes

Now that we understand the relevance of subtypes, let's explore how the content and process of OCD operate within the common subtypes we've introduced. After each subtype, you'll notice two things: (1) a statement about the OCD process with blank spaces to fill in and (2) an obsessive-compulsive cycle diagram with blanks to complete. By filling these out, you'll get a firmer grasp of the cycle you've been caught in so that you can effectively identify it, interrupt it, and escape its grip.

You probably won't personally relate to all the subtypes. If one doesn't resonate for you, you *can* skip it, though I would encourage you to fill out at least one example that is unrelated to your obsessions. Considering examples that aren't particularly triggering to you will help you develop clarity about the process and more effectively intervene when your own obsessions arise. Use the descriptions provided to fill in the blanks with sample obsessions and compulsions and reflect on the similarities to your own obsessions and mental compulsions.

The first blank asks for your "trigger," which is something that precedes and incites the obsession. A trigger may be external, a person, place, or thing, or it may be internal, a sensation, emotion, or even another obsession like an intrusive image. If you can't identify a trigger, you can leave it blank. The emotion section might involve many feelings, though anxiety, doubt, guilt, shame, discomfort, disgust, and distress are common in OCD.

In the space after the phrase "I wanted to," write down a compulsion. While this OCD process statement and the tools throughout this book apply to all types of compulsions, I encourage you to focus on and write down mental compulsions. This will help you develop your awareness of internal behaviors.

Scrupulosity OCD

Individuals with this subtype usually feel fear and guilt about whether they are morally righteous. Religious scrupulosity involves rigidity about following an established religious code whereas moral scrupulosity focuses on adherence to an individual moral code. In both forms of scrupulosity, the passive, obsessive thoughts center on concerns about being moral or faithful enough.

Religious Scrupulosity

Religious scrupulosity can involve sacrilegious images or thoughts like *I love the devil.* Some with this subtype worry that their thoughts will impact their salvation. Others experience doubt about whether their actions align with their faith's teachings. They may fear they have misinterpreted religious texts or worry about the authenticity of their devotion. They may be triggered if they disagree with an authority figure. They may find that reading scripture and praying are anxiety-provoking.

Typically, those with this subtype fear God's judgment and wrath. They seek an absolute understanding of religious tenets and attempt to implement them perfectly. They may feel scared they'll get "caught on a technicality" if they don't correctly interpret and follow the rules of their faith.

If you have religious scrupulosity, you might perform mental compulsions like:

- Internally debating religious doctrine to try to determine whether an action is "right" or "wrong."
- Praying repeatedly to ensure the prayer is "just right."
- Thinking a good thought about God to cancel out a bad thought.
- Emotionally checking to see how you feel about God and if your faith is authentic.
- Mentally reassuring yourself by repeating phrases. For instance, if you are worried about the possibility of going to hell because of sacrilegious thoughts, you might repeatedly tell yourself "God knows my heart."
- Beating up on yourself to atone for potential or actual wrongdoings.

OCD Process Statement

__________________ led to __________________________________.
a triggered occurred — an obsession (intrusive thought, image, urge, emotion, or "What if?"

The obsession made me feel __________________________________.
an emotion (e.g. amxiety, doubt, distress, guilt, shame, discomfort, disgust)

In response to the thought and feeling, I wanted to __________________________.
perform a compulsion

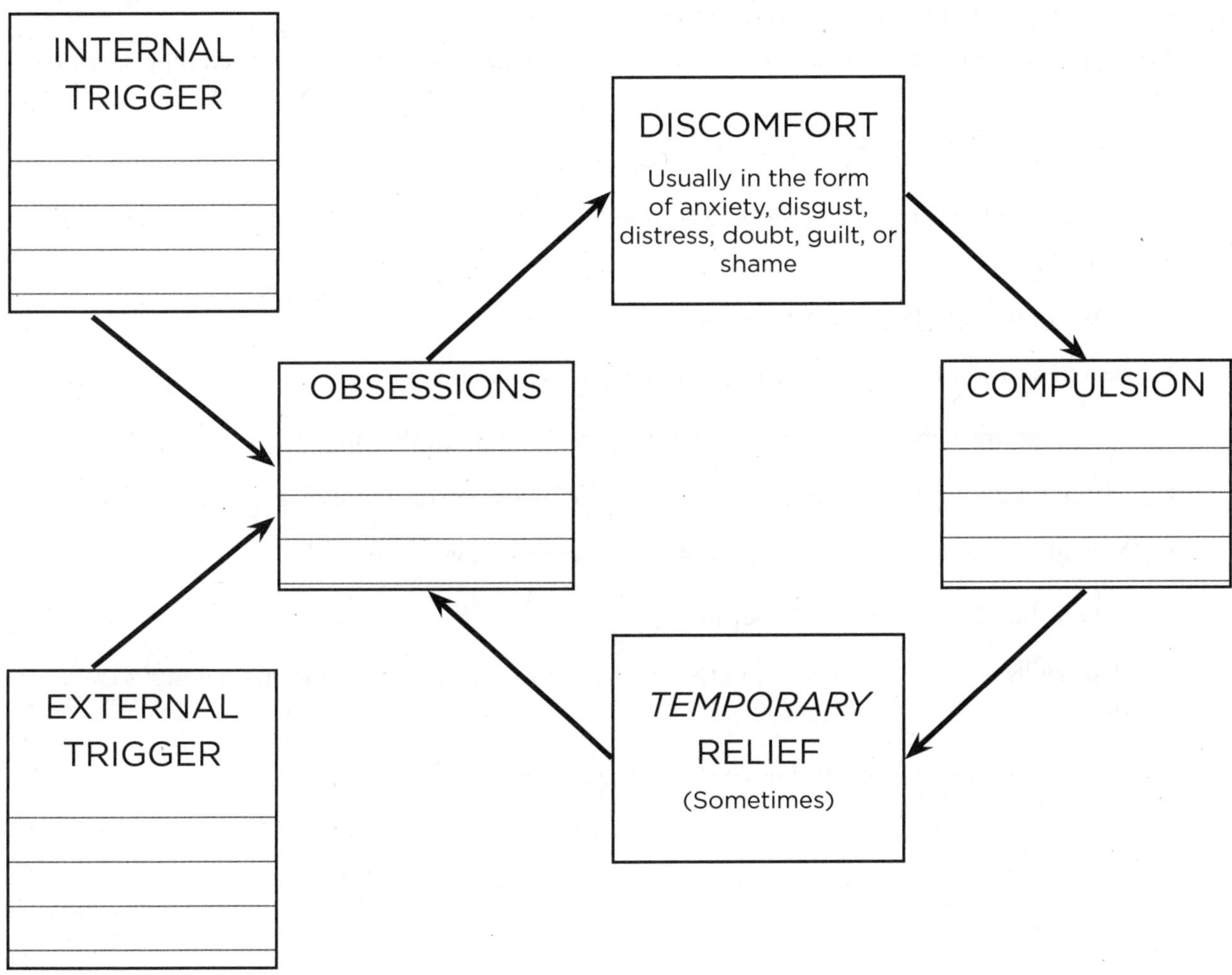

Moral Scrupulosity

Those with moral scrupulosity are fixated on perfectly adhering to moral ideals—honesty, kindness, loyalty, and the like. While most people aspire to these characteristics, the rigid way that those with moral scrupulosity attempt to stick to their values becomes problematic. They want to ensure they're *perfectly* meeting their own moral standards.

Some with this subtype fear they might be outcast because of some potential misstep. Given this, cancel culture is often a trigger for those with moral scrupulosity. Others with moral scrupulosity are concerned about living their lives authentically lest they be hypocritical. Some become morally scrupulous about an established moral code. For instance, members of twelve-step groups sometimes experience concerns about being perfectly aligned with the program.

Attempts to resolve doubt about morality take various forms. Those who are worried they might have offended someone may:

- Scan people's faces to check if they seem offended.
- Try to recall exactly what they said to another person to ensure they didn't say anything inappropriate.
- Mentally debate whether a behavior was offensive.
- Search for holes in memories that could indicate a blackout.

If they're concerned about whether they're being perfectly honest, they might:

- Check their emotions to see if they "feel like" they're expressing themselves authentically.
- Mentally review past situations to ensure they remember events correctly.

If they fear that they were unkind, they might:

- Repeatedly reassure themselves that their actions were necessary, and it wasn't "wrong" to take those actions.
- Excessively analyze whether they owe someone an apology.

OCD Process Statement

______________________ led to ______________________________________.
a triggered occurred — an obsession (intrusive thought, image, urge, emotion, or "What if?"

The obsession made me feel ______________________________________.
an emotion (e.g. amxiety, doubt, distress, guilt, shame, discomfort, disgust)

In response to the thought and feeling, I wanted to ______________________________.
perform a compulsion

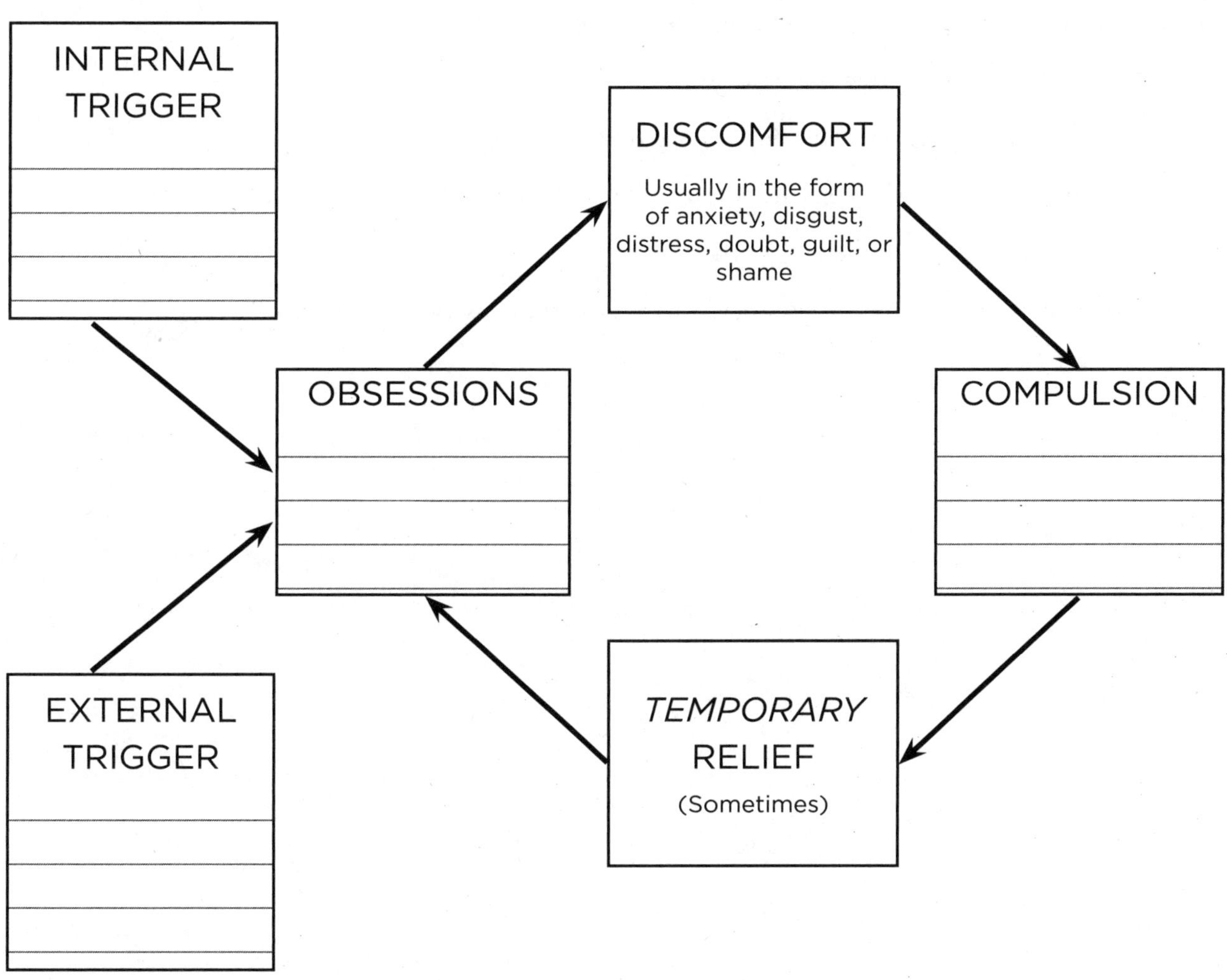

Real Event OCD

This subtype could be viewed as a form of moral scrupulosity about a past event given that those with this theme often worry that some behavior in their past is unforgivable. Many with real event OCD fear they don't have OCD because their concerns are related to an event that actually transpired. They may say things like "This can't be OCD because it actually happened!"

But everyone does things they regret and only some respond to such regrets excessively. While people generally choose to stop persecuting themselves over the past at some point, individuals with real event OCD become preoccupied with an all-or-none perspective of an experience and have difficulty making a definitive choice to put the past to rest.

People with this subtype agonize over what an event might mean about them and whether they have properly atoned for their behavior. They might respond by:

- Ruminating about if they are "bad" people.
- Mentally reviewing the experience to determine their intent.
- Mentally debating whether others would forgive or shun them if they knew.
- Excessively reassuring themselves they aren't bad.
- Beating themselves up because they don't believe they deserve to be happy.

OCD Process Statement

________________ led to ______________________________.
a triggered occurred an obsession (intrusive thought, image, urge, emotion, or "What if?"

The obsession made me feel ______________________________.
an emotion (e.g. amxiety, doubt, distress, guilt, shame, discomfort, disgust)

In response to the thought and feeling, I wanted to ______________________________.
perform a compulsion

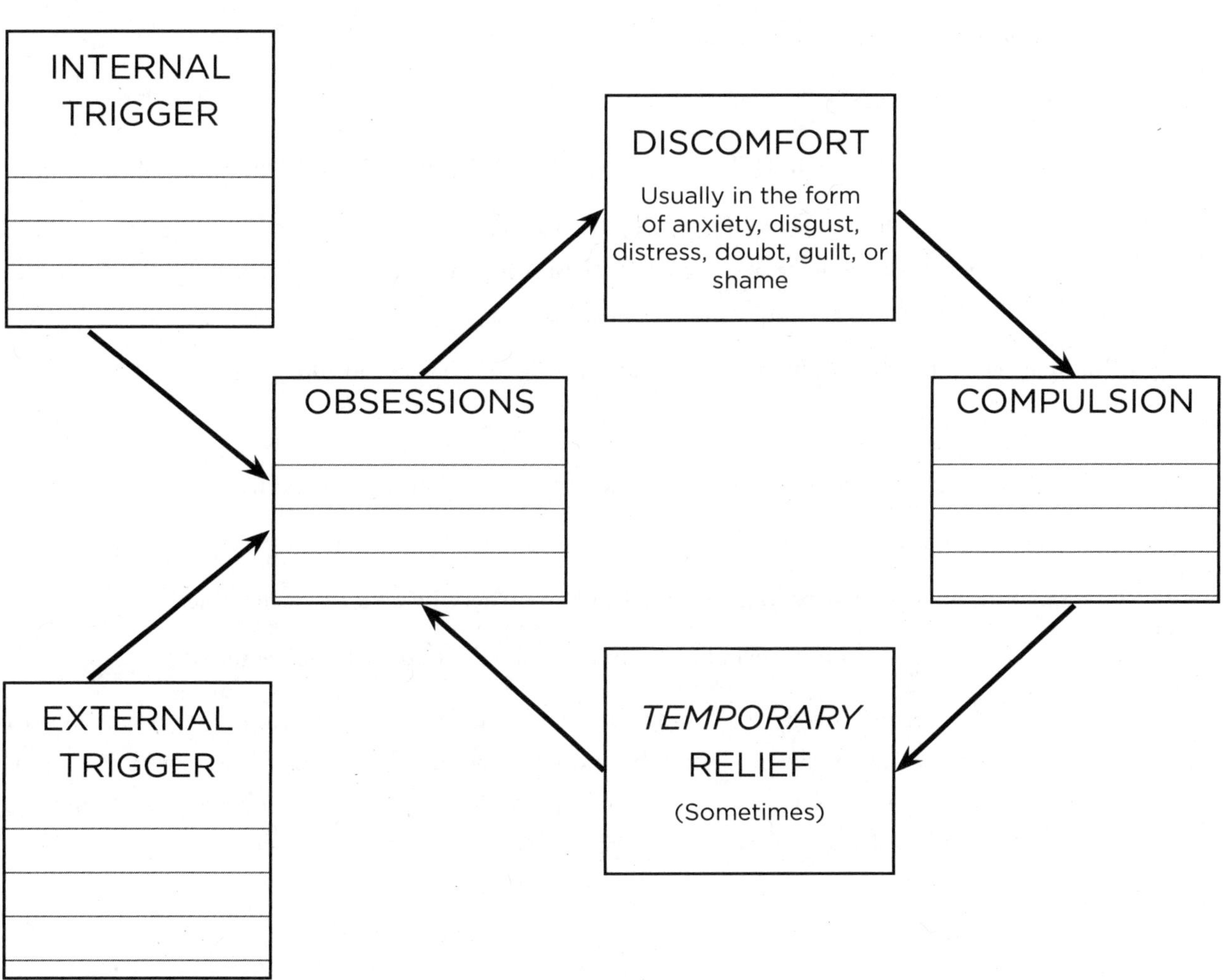

Relationship OCD

Relationship OCD (ROCD) involves fears about the quality of a relationship or partner. While this subtype can attack *any* type of relationship, we'll focus on obsessions about intimate partnerships here.

Interacting with romantic partner(s) and people, generally, can trigger people with ROCD. This means that work, errands, social events, film, television, and social media are teeming with triggers. These triggers lead those with ROCD to question the "rightness" of their partner or relationship. They may wonder if feelings of annoyance, boredom, or frustration are signs of a "bad" relationship. They might struggle with intrusive images of infidelity. They might have thoughts like:

I'm not feeling love toward my partner right now. What does that mean?

I don't always like my partner's sense of humor. Maybe they're not "the one."

I just noticed an attractive person. I could be unfaithful!

My partner and I get into arguments or don't agree on some issues. Maybe they're abusive or bad for me.

Those with this theme often worry that they will live a subpar, unhappy life as a direct result of making the "wrong" choice about staying in or leaving their relationship. To prevent making the "wrong" choice, people with ROCD often perform mental compulsions like:

- Ruminating about what an interaction indicates about their relationship.
- Checking if they feel love.
- Excessively reassuring themselves that it's okay if their relationship isn't perfect.
- Mentally debating whether the relationship is "right."
- Mentally reviewing scenarios to determine if their partner's behavior is acceptable.
- Checking physical sensations, including groinal sensations, to determine degree of attraction.

Relationship OCD can also involve fear thoughts related to how someone you're in a relationship with feels about you. While fear of negative evaluation by another may seem like social anxiety or basic insecurity, the differences between these are somewhat arbitrary, and the function of behaviors is usually the same. Given this, it doesn't substantively affect our approach.

OCD Process Statement

_______________ led to _______________.
a triggered occurred — an obsession (intrusive thought, image, urge, emotion, or "What if?"

The obsession made me feel _______________.
an emotion (e.g. amxiety, doubt, distress, guilt, shame, discomfort, disgust)

In response to the thought and feeling, I wanted to _______________.
perform a compulsion

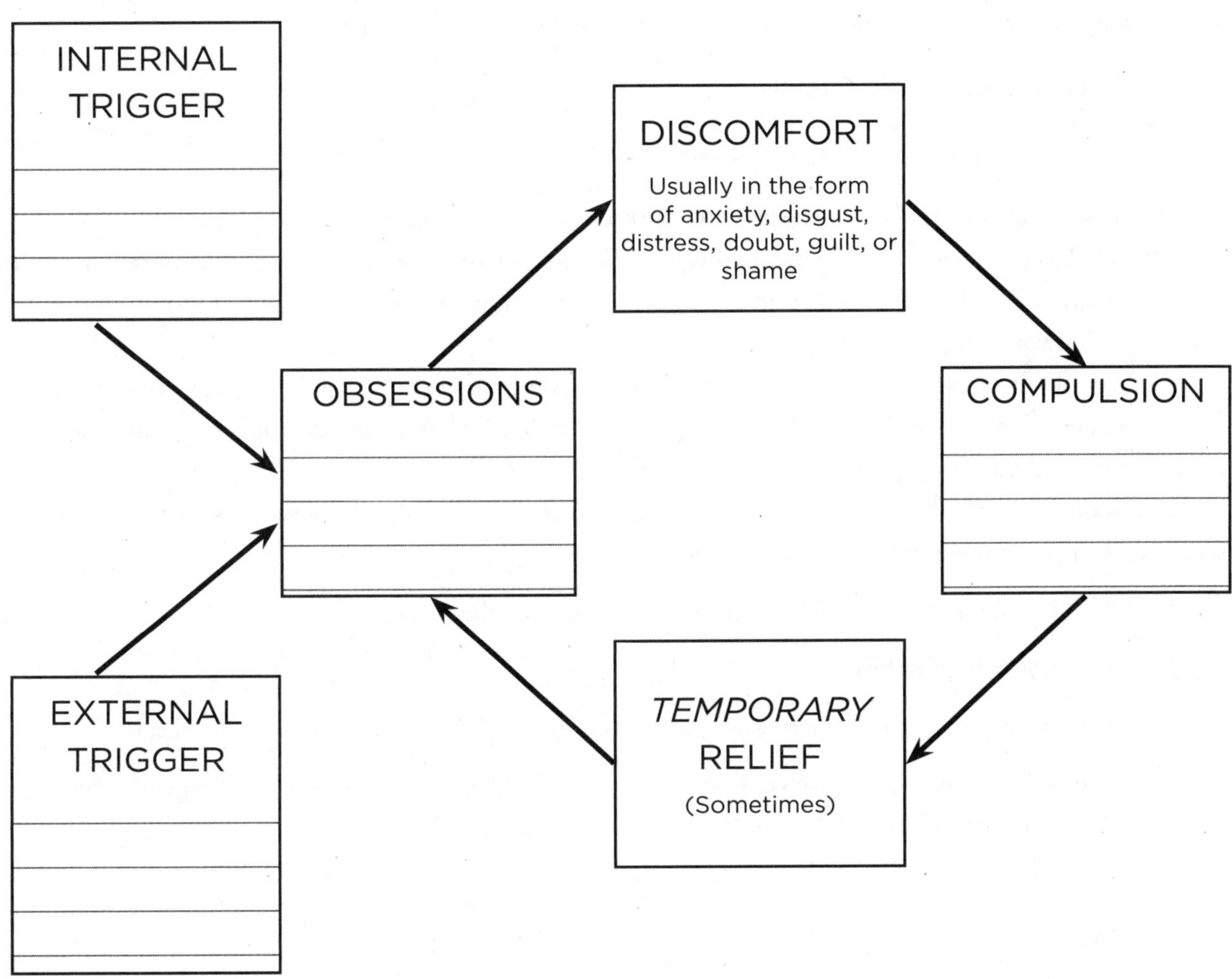

Sexual Orientation OCD

This subtype can impact anyone of any sexual orientation. Individuals with this theme are usually concerned that they aren't identified with their authentic or "true" sexual orientation. So, if someone identifies as gay, they might fear that they are really straight, bisexual, or pansexual.

People with this subtype are often triggered by sensations in their groins and try desperately to determine what their physical sensations mean about their preferences. They usually find media content related to love and attraction to be anxiety-provoking as it invites questions about whether they find the content arousing. Many with this theme experience explicit images. Some experience thoughts like:

What if I'm not really (straight, gay, bi, pan)?

What if I'm lying to myself and I later realize I've been in denial this whole time?

What if I hurt people because I'm wrong?

What if I'm missing out on something that would make me truly happy?

Simply looking at people is often triggering to those with sexual orientation OCD. So, while scrolling on social media, you might see an individual you think you *shouldn't* feel attraction to and worry that you *do* feel attraction. While in line at the store, you may see a person you believe you *should* feel attraction to and worry that you don't.

Anxiety about attraction occurs both in SO-OCD and relationship OCD, and these two subtypes often co-occur. Someone may worry that they are in the "wrong" relationship specifically because they are identified inauthentically as gay, straight, bi, and so forth.

In response to their concerns about being identified inauthentically, people with sexual orientation OCD tend to perform mental compulsions like:

- Checking physical sensations like groinal movements or heart rate.
- Checking feelings of love.
- Mentally reviewing interactions and sexual encounters to determine degree of attraction.
- Repeatedly reassuring themselves that they are attracted to the gender(s) that align with their identified sexual orientation.

OCD Process Statement

_______________ led to _______________.
a triggered occurred — an obsession (intrusive thought, image, urge, emotion, or "What if?"

The obsession made me feel _______________.
an emotion (e.g. amxiety, doubt, distress, guilt, shame, discomfort, disgust)

In response to the thought and feeling, I wanted to _______________.
perform a compulsion

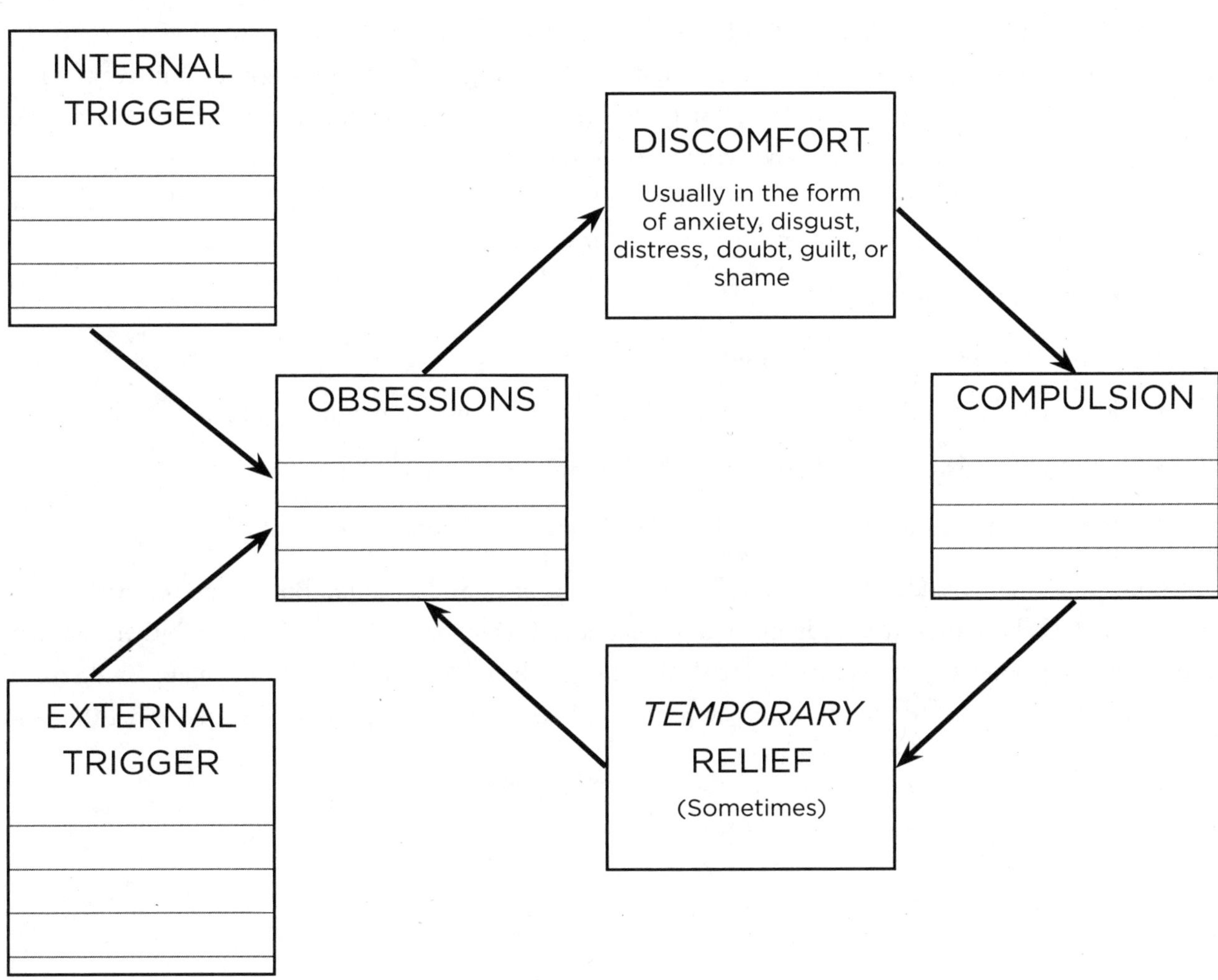

Existential OCD

Questions of existence are the centerpiece of this subtype, and related obsessions run the gamut. Specific fears often revolve around the afterlife, the meaning of life, and the nature of reality. Some with this subtype worry that they are actually dead. Others may fear they are living in a coma, a dream, a simulation, or even the matrix.

You may wonder why we would classify philosophizing as OCD. There's nothing inherently wrong with pondering such questions on existence, just like there's nothing wrong with reflecting on your relationship or your sexuality. OCD is only relevant when the behaviors aimed at addressing related distress become consuming.

People who are anxious about whether reality is as it appears are often triggered by feelings of derealization and depersonalization. Depersonalization involves a sense of being removed from yourself or your body. Derealization involves a sense of detachment that can be interpreted as things not feeling "real." I use quotation marks because, ultimately, "real" isn't a feeling. What people with derealization experience are *judgments* of how their current experience compares to their preferred state.

When people with existential OCD are triggered, whether by derealization, talk of the afterlife, or reading about someone in a coma, they often perform mental compulsions like:

- Checking to see if things "feel real."
- Reassuring themselves that they aren't living in a dream.
- Reviewing memories to determine if their memories are authentic or manufactured.
- Ruminating about the likelihood that reality is different than it appears.
- Scenario twisting to determine how they might feel in different imagined afterlives.

Some might see this idea—that reality is not as it appears—as delusional. But the person with OCD doesn't wholly believe that they are living in a simulation, a dream, or an alternate reality. Rather, they are fearful that they *could* be. Someone who is delusional would be convinced they were living in an alternate reality and would live as though this reality were the truth. Someone with OCD feels scared about the possibility that reality is not as it appears to be.

OCD Process Statement

____________________ led to ____.
a triggered occurred an obsession (intrusive thought, image, urge, emotion, or "What if?"

The obsession made me feel ____.
an emotion (e.g. amxiety, doubt, distress, guilt, shame, discomfort, disgust)

In response to the thought and feeling, I wanted to ______________________________.
perform a compulsion

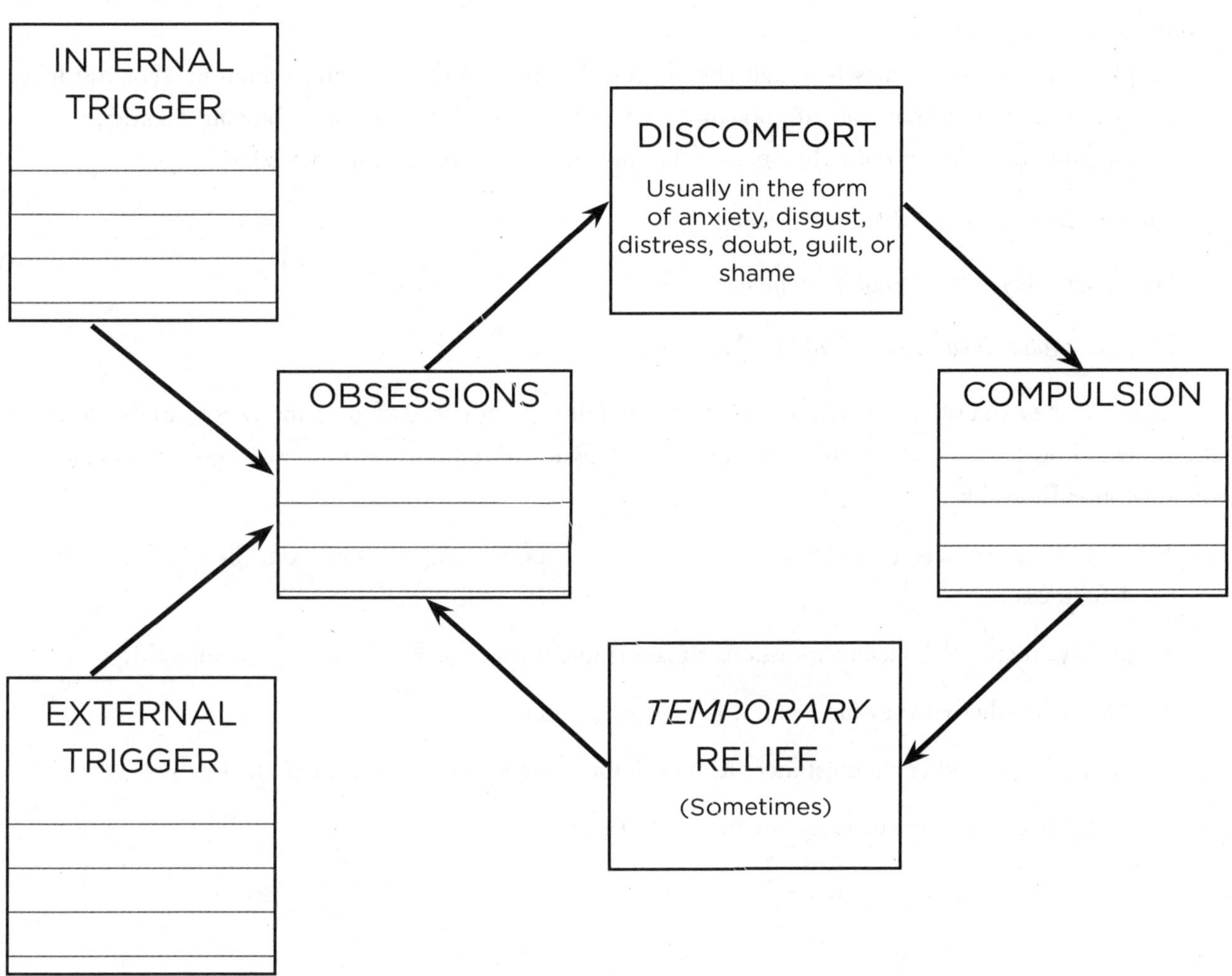

Mental Health OCD

Mental health obsessions involve fears that one might unknowingly have or could develop a mental illness. Oftentimes, people with this subtype struggle with anxiety about psychosis. Their obsessions might sound like:

I just heard a sound. Am I hallucinating?

I just saw something out of the corner of my eye. Am I seeing things?

What if I develop psychosis and am unable to care for myself?

They may also experience thoughts that sound like commands and worry that these are command hallucinations.

People with this theme may fear that they have other mental illnesses and symptoms. For instance, some experience anxiety that they unknowingly have or will develop depression, bipolar disorder, narcissistic personality disorder, or borderline personality disorder. Their obsessions may sound like:

I'm sad. Does that mean that I'm depressed?

I'm feeling really happy. What if I'm manic?

I'm feeling good about myself. Could I be a narcissist?

This list isn't exhaustive. There are so many mental illnesses and therefore so many potential obsessions about mental health. In response to these thoughts, people with mental health obsessions often engage in mental compulsions like:

- Checking feelings to determine if they are experiencing an emotion, like sadness or happiness.
- Analyzing people's facial expressions to determine if other people heard or saw something.
- Debating whether they meet certain diagnostic criteria.
- Mentally reviewing circumstances to determine if their behavior was mentally healthy.
- Thinking of happy memories any time they feel sad to neutralize sadness.

OCD Process Statement

____________________ led to ______________________________________.
a triggered occurred an obsession (intrusive thought, image, urge, emotion, or "What if?"

The obsession made me feel ______________________________________.
an emotion (e.g. amxiety, doubt, distress, guilt, shame, discomfort, disgust)

In response to the thought and feeling, I wanted to ______________________________.
perform a compulsion

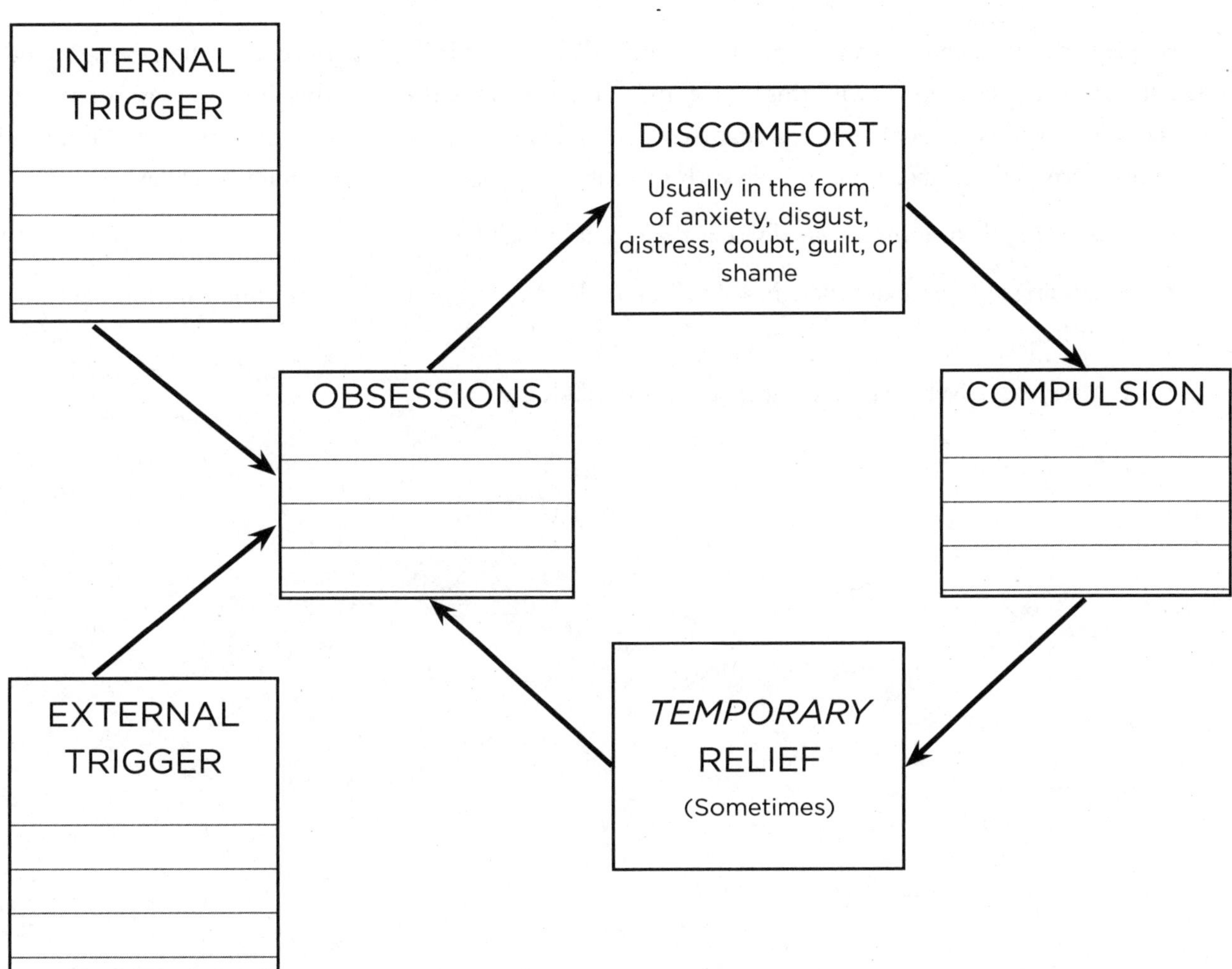

Self-Harm OCD

Those with self-harm OCD are generally worried that they might want to take their own lives. Obsessions can include graphic images of suicide and concerns about what such images mean. Fear can arise when someone is feeling sad or somehow struggling. What if thoughts may include:

What if I feel unhappy forever and have no choice but to kill myself?

What if I want to kill myself now and don't realize it?

I just had a thought about death. Does that mean I don't want to live?

What if I end my life and, because of this, I go to hell?

People with this theme often find media coverage of suicides to be highly triggering. The experience of OCD itself can also be a trigger with this theme. Indeed, those in the throes of this disorder may worry that their condition will never get better and that they could, therefore, want to end their lives in the future.

In response to these obsessions, people with this subtype perform mental compulsions like:

- Reassuring themselves repeatedly that they wouldn't self-harm.
- Analyzing feelings about thoughts of suicide to determine whether they genuinely want to end their lives.
- Praying excessively to protect against urges to self-harm.

OCD Process Statement

____________________ led to ____.
a triggered occurred — an obsession (intrusive thought, image, urge, emotion, or "What if?"

The obsession made me feel ____.
an emotion (e.g. amxiety, doubt, distress, guilt, shame, discomfort, disgust)

In response to the thought and feeling, I wanted to ____________________________.
perform a compulsion

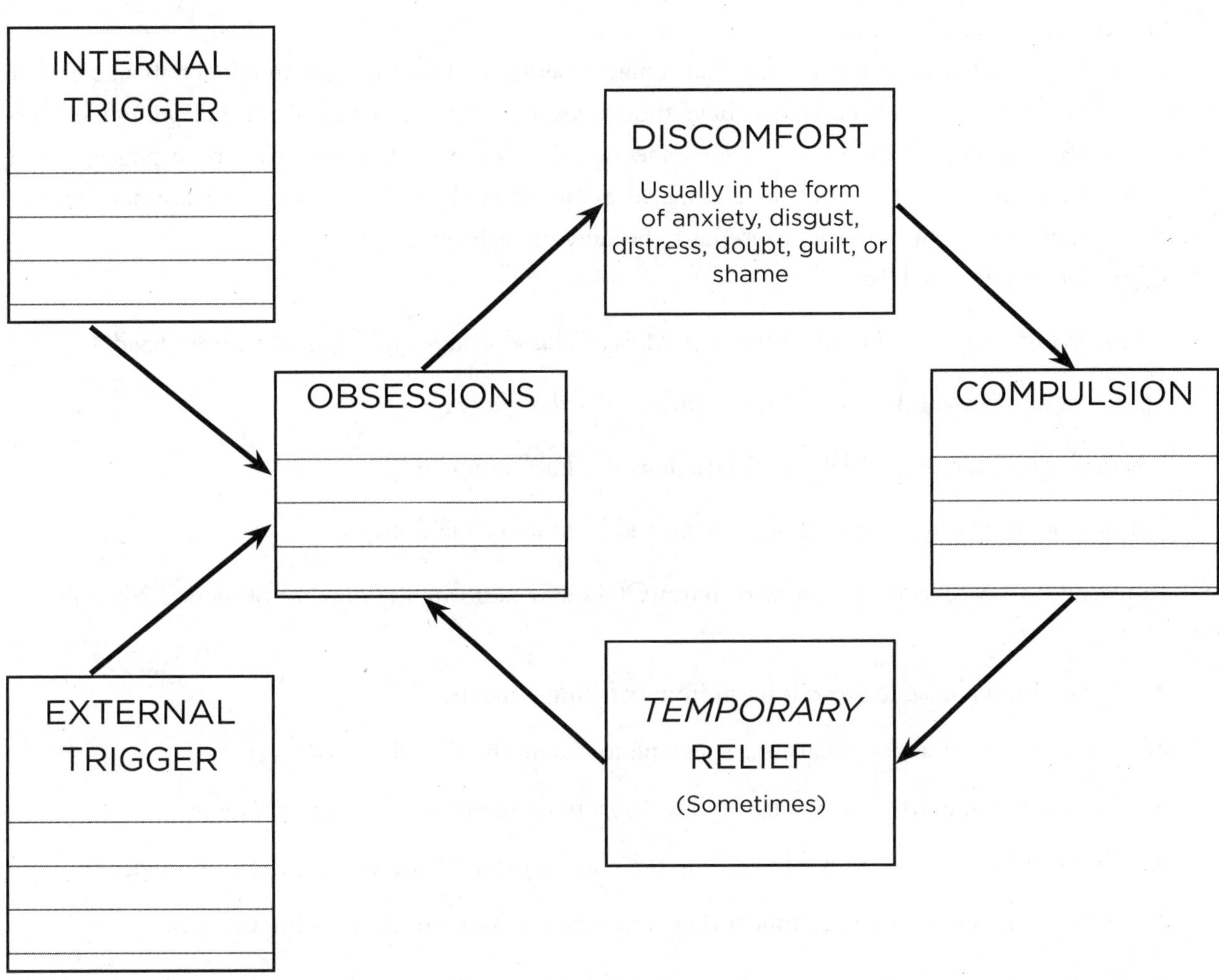

Harm OCD

Some people with harm-related obsessions fear that harm will befall themselves or their loved ones. They may, for example, worry about home invasions or natural disasters. Obsessions might include images of a violent bank robbery or thoughts like *What if my cat were in an earthquake and got trapped under the rubble?*

While harm OCD can involve fears about passively being harmed, this theme often involves fears of *causing* harm. The key word here is *fears*. These are NOT individuals who have a plan or genuine desire to cause harm. People with harm-related obsessions find harm-related thoughts upsetting. Some might wonder, *How do I know whether my thoughts upset me? Maybe they don't! Maybe I don't have OCD?* Notice that this still involves doubt about the enjoyment of thoughts and the desire to cause harm. This doubt is different from a clear plan to cause harm.

Some people with fears of perpetrating harm may experience violent images and doubt about whether they could perpetrate such an act. Others have thoughts appear in their minds like *Kill them!* and feel terrified that they might secretly want to take someone's life. Some really enjoy true crime podcasts and wonder, *What does it mean that I like these so much?* Some worry they will deliberately cause harm, while others fear that they might indirectly cause harm because of negligence.

Obsessions often sound like:

I didn't feel remorse for cutting that person off. Maybe I'm a sociopath, and I'll murder my husband.

I just imagined stabbing my sister. Was that an intrusive thought or a fantasy?

I thought about dropping my child out the window. Am I a danger to her?

I think I saw something in my peripheral vision. Did I hit someone with my car?

In response to obsessions, people with harm OCD may perform any number of mental compulsions like:

- Repeating a phrase to prevent harm from befalling someone.
- Bringing up a thought of harming someone to ensure the thought causes fear.
- Reviewing times when they were kind to reassure themselves about their character.
- Excessively scanning the road to ensure there aren't objects that might lead to an accident.
- Rehearsing how they would cope if they were arrested for committing a hit-and-run.

While many with harm OCD worry that they could take someone else's life, others fear that they could be violent even if that violence doesn't cause death. They might worry that they raped someone in the past or that they will sexually prey on their pet.

OCD Process Statement

________________ led to ________________________________.
a triggered occurred — an obsession (intrusive thought, image, urge, emotion, or "What if?"

The obsession made me feel ________________________________.
an emotion (e.g. amxiety, doubt, distress, guilt, shame, discomfort, disgust)

In response to the thought and feeling, I wanted to ________________________.
perform a compulsion

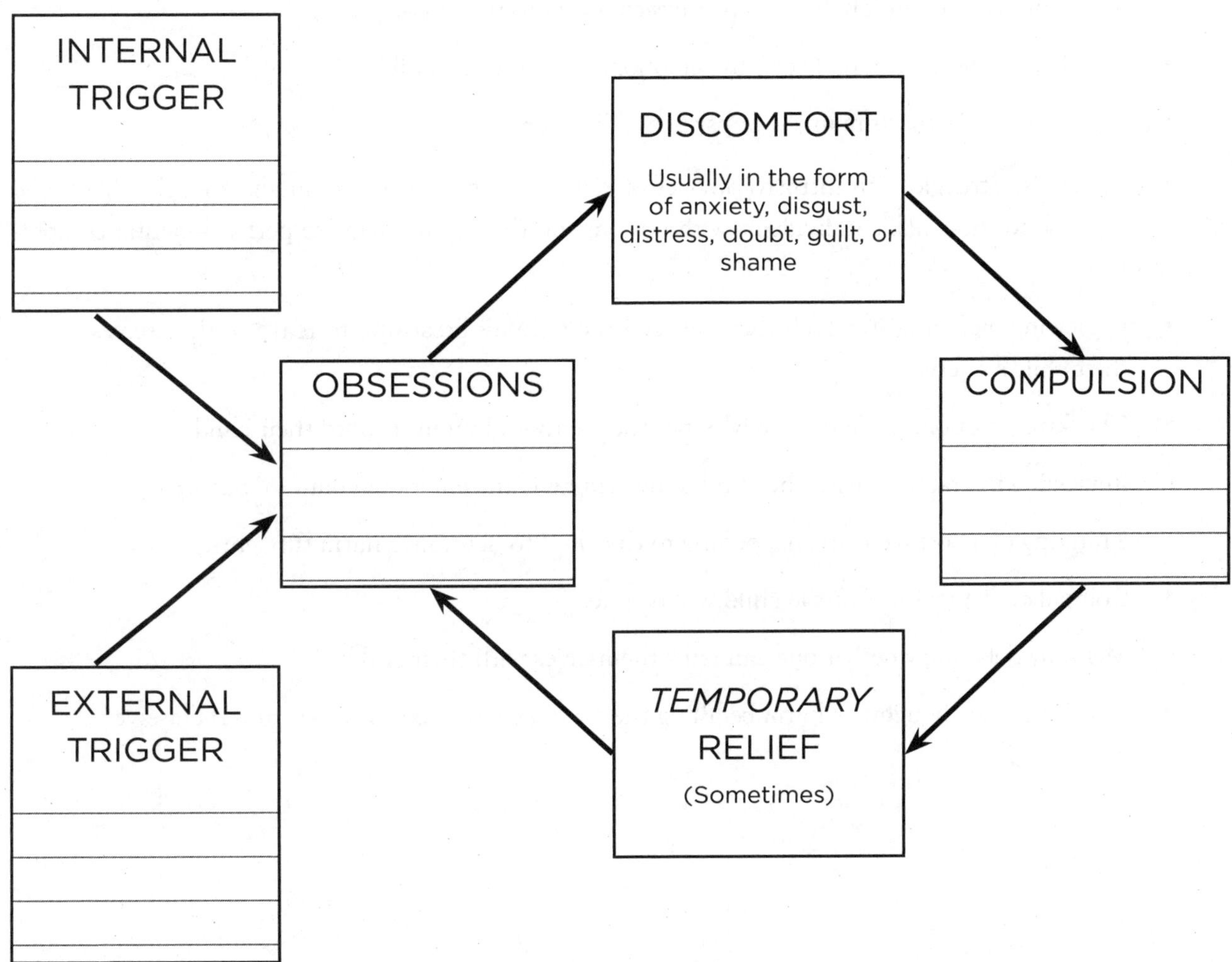

Postpartum-Themed OCD

Like postpartum depression, postpartum OCD refers to OCD symptoms that begin during the postpartum period. Indeed, some people who carry children first experience obsessions during pregnancy or following delivery, and partners of those carrying children are not exempt from struggles during this time.

In addition to the postpartum *onset* of OCD, there are also obsessional themes that are commonly experienced by new parents. Here, I'll be talking about the content that commonly arises during the perinatal and postpartum periods. Ultimately, though, any obsessions can arise during pregnancy or after birth.

New parents with perinatal and postpartum obsessions are often concerned about:

- Their child dying unexpectedly.
- Accidentally or intentionally causing physical harm to the child.
- Accidentally or intentionally causing emotional harm to the child.
- Experiencing postpartum mood or psychotic disorders.

They may also struggle with intrusive images of causing harm or with command thoughts like *Drop him!* In response to these fears, individuals with postpartum themes are likely to perform mental compulsions like:

- Reviewing memories in which they checked their child's breathing to reassure themselves of their child's safety.
- Checking emotions to determine whether they harbor ill intent toward their child.
- Reviewing interactions with the child to determine if any emotional damage occurred.
- Thinking of a positive thing happening to the child to neutralize harm thoughts.
- Compulsively praying that the child will be safe.
- Mentally debating whether one can trust themselves with their child.
- Checking that thoughts of harm befalling their child cause anxiety to reassure themselves.

OCD Process Statement

_______________ led to _______________________________.
a triggered occurred — an obsession (intrusive thought, image, urge, emotion, or "What if?"

The obsession made me feel _______________________________.
an emotion (e.g. amxiety, doubt, distress, guilt, shame, discomfort, disgust)

In response to the thought and feeling, I wanted to _______________________________.
perform a compulsion

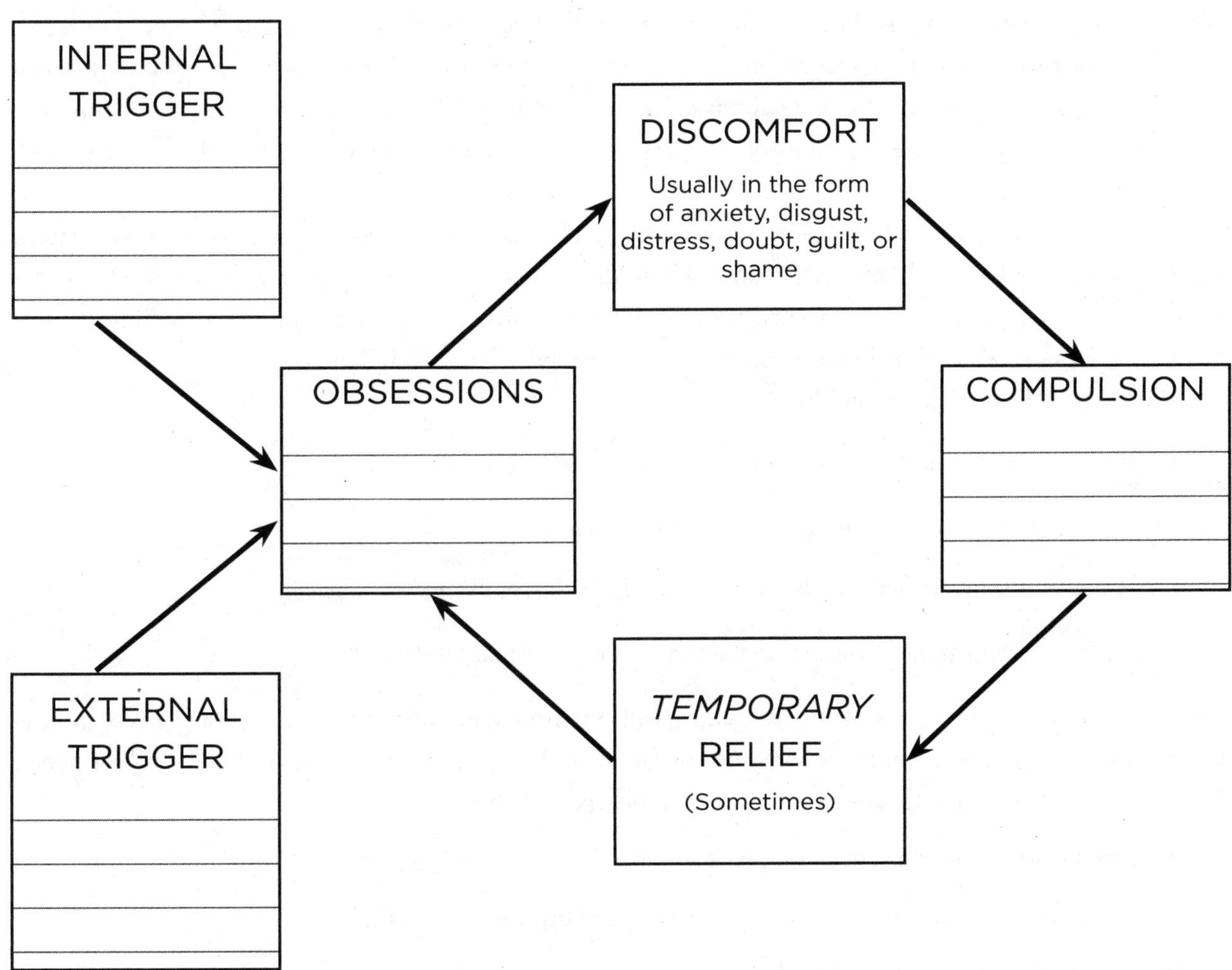

Pedophilia-Themed OCD

Pedophilia-themed OCD (POCD) is a very specific form of harm OCD that involves fears about causing harm to children. It's critical to be clear here: having obsessions about whether you're attracted to or could harm a child is different from being attracted to or harming a child. The difference between having pedophilia-related obsessions and being a pedophile is like the difference between worrying about whether you want to harm somebody and having a plan to murder someone.

You may wonder why there is an entire section dedicated to this theme if we've already talked about the larger category of Harm OCD. It is my hope that giving pedophilia-themed OCD its own subsection will support people with this subtype in experiencing less shame.

I don't mean to diminish other people's experience. Shame occurs in other subtypes. It's not easy to admit to the presence of many thoughts, and it's understandable why those with other subtypes are secretive, too. But pedophiles are arguably among the most loathed and outcast population, making fears of being shunned by society all the more intense for those with POCD. By casting a light on pedophilia-themed OCD, we reduce the stigma associated with these obsessions, and, hopefully, help people to seek treatment more readily.

Some people with POCD experience unwanted, graphic images of touching children inappropriately. Please take note of the word "unwanted" here. These thoughts are upsetting to people with POCD. It's also worth noting that people can experience doubt over whether the thoughts are actually upsetting. Again, this doubt about whether they like the images is different than definitively liking them.

"What if" thoughts may sound like:

I noticed that child is pretty. Am I attracted to her?

Why do images of a baby's penis keep popping into my mind?

I played doctor with another kid when I was a kid. Does that make me a pedophile?

I touched my child's genitals while changing their diaper. Was that intentional?

Terrified of what others might think, people will suffer for years without talking about or researching their symptoms. Given this, mental compulsions factor heavily into the experience of pedophilia-themed OCD. Some common mental compulsions in this subtype include:

- Scanning the body to check for physical sensations after seeing a child.
- Ruminating about whether an early sexual experience was inappropriate.
- Comparing the love felt toward children to the love felt in intimate partnerships.
- Mentally debating whether an image is truly unwanted.
- Reviewing instances in which one was kind toward a child as a form of reassurance.

OCD Process Statement

______________________ led to ____.
a triggered occurred — an obsession (intrusive thought, image, urge, emotion, or "What if?"

The obsession made me feel ____.
an emotion (e.g. amxiety, doubt, distress, guilt, shame, discomfort, disgust)

In response to the thought and feeling, I wanted to ________________________________.
perform a compulsion

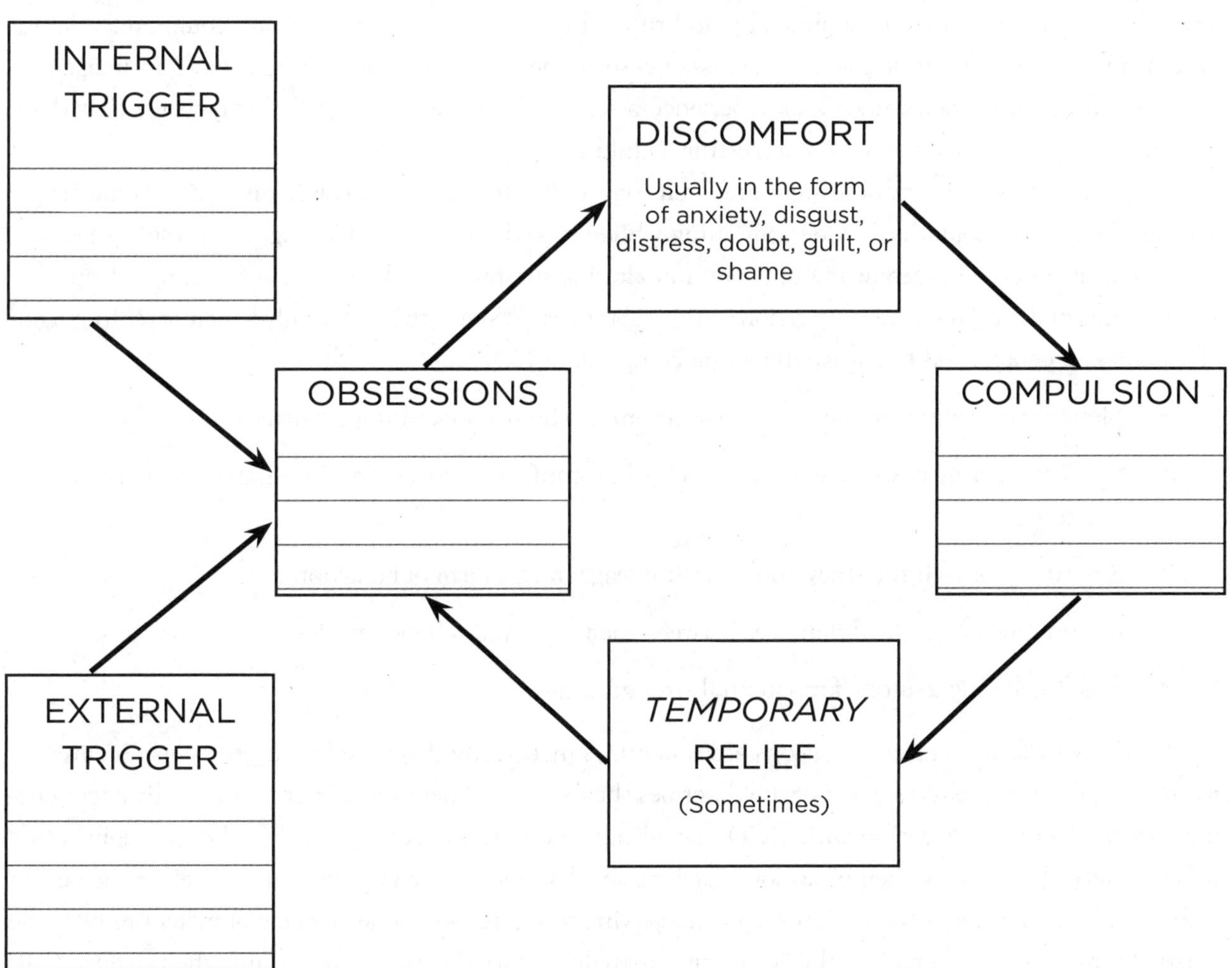

False Memory OCD

People with false memory OCD experience doubt about whether thoughts and images in their minds could be actual memories of events that occurred. Sometimes, the thought or image is completely random. For example, you could have a thought that, at some point, you blurted out something offensive. A thought or image could also be connected to a memory that you're confident happened. For example, a violent image could jump into your mind in a familiar setting like a party you attended.

This is where real event and false memory OCD can collide. You might have a clear memory of being drunk at a party and feel guilty about how drunk you got (real event OCD) and then wonder if images you visualize in the context of this party are memories (false memory OCD).

Oftentimes, these "memories" involve being the victim or perpetrator of a morally reprehensible behavior. Topics like rape, murder, pedophilia, hit-and-runs, cheating, lying, and stealing are common fodder for false memory OCD. When it comes to obsessions, someone with this subtype might have an image of a naked child pop into their minds and experience a sensation in their groin. They may worry that these sensations or images are a memory of molesting a child.

People with false memory obsessions are often triggered by the idea of repressed memories. Some people are afraid that they could have done something while blacked out or sleepwalking. As a result, they may completely avoid even moderate amounts of mind-altering substances or have difficulty falling asleep.

In terms of doubt, the central question of this subtype is "What if this is actually a memory?" In pursuit of the answer, people tend to engage in mental compulsions like:

- Mentally reviewing circumstances to determine whether something occurred.
- Comparing a memory that someone else has confirmed to be true with the "memory" in question.
- Reassuring oneself that they could never engage in this form of behavior.
- Ruminating about the differences between memories and false memories.
- Self-flagellating to atone for potential wrongdoings.

People with false memory obsessions are sometimes incorrectly diagnosed with psychosis. A clinician might fail to properly assess someone who describes themselves as "delusional" but isn't actually experiencing clinical delusions. A person with OCD may also be more deeply convinced that their thoughts *could* reflect reality, thus making their obsessions appear to be delusional. The key question is whether the person is focused on doubt. Does the person spend time trying to figure out the legitimacy of memories or is the person living their lives as though the "memories" actually occurred without questioning their reality at all?

OCD Process Statement

_______________ led to _______________.
a triggered occurred — an obsession (intrusive thought, image, urge, emotion, or "What if?"

The obsession made me feel _______________.
an emotion (e.g. amxiety, doubt, distress, guilt, shame, discomfort, disgust)

In response to the thought and feeling, I wanted to _______________.
perform a compulsion

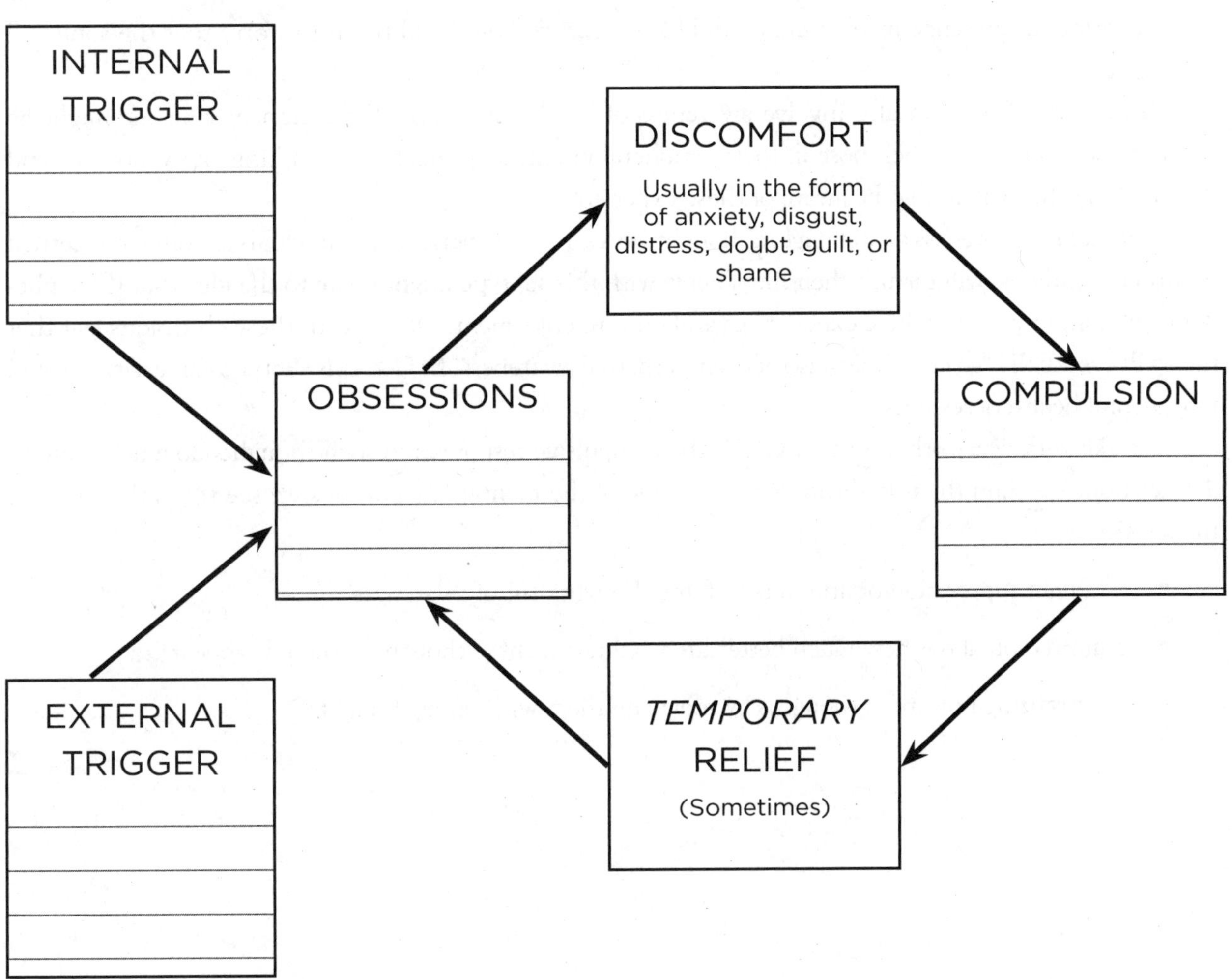

Hyperawareness OCD

Hyperawareness OCD involves distress about a heightened degree of awareness of an experience. Sometimes we refer to obsessions in this subtype as neutral obsessions. While these obsessions are anything but neutral to those experiencing them, the content of the thoughts may be considered neutral as it isn't inherently upsetting. For instance, you might see a billboard on the freeway advertising gum. While the billboard itself isn't offensive, the image of that billboard may continuously flash into your awareness. Over time, you might be troubled by the presence of that image and the idea that it could continue to be lodged in your mind. It's the involuntary thoughts of the billboard and the idea that these thoughts could continue that disturb those with neutral obsessions.

This distress can attach to thoughts. For instance, you could get a song stuck in your head, and the song's continuous presence in your mind could be intrusive. You could begin to worry that the song will never go away.

Neutral obsessions can also involve awareness of bodily sensations. For instance, someone might be upset by the awareness of their nose in their peripheral vision, their breathing, blinking, or swallowing, and the idea that they will always be aware of these experiences.

Whether it's awareness of an image, a thought, or a sensory experience, individuals are often concerned that their awareness will tarnish their life. People with this subtype might relate to the idea that these phenomena "contaminate" positive experiences and prevent enjoyment. Others with these obsessions fear that they will eventually "go crazy" because of their perpetual awareness. In fact, this subtype can easily dovetail into mental health obsessions.

Just like with every other form of OCD, the compulsive responses to such thoughts do much more to detract from life than the initial thoughts do. Some of the mental compulsions we see regularly with this theme include:

- Thought suppression or attempts to force thoughts out of awareness.
- Rumination about how much better life would be if these thoughts would disappear.
- Neutralizing unwanted thoughts by replacing them with other thoughts.

OCD Process Statement

________________ led to ____________________________.
a triggered occurred — an obsession (intrusive thought, image, urge, emotion, or "What if?"

The obsession made me feel ____________________________.
an emotion (e.g. amxiety, doubt, distress, guilt, shame, discomfort, disgust)

In response to the thought and feeling, I wanted to ____________________.
perform a compulsion

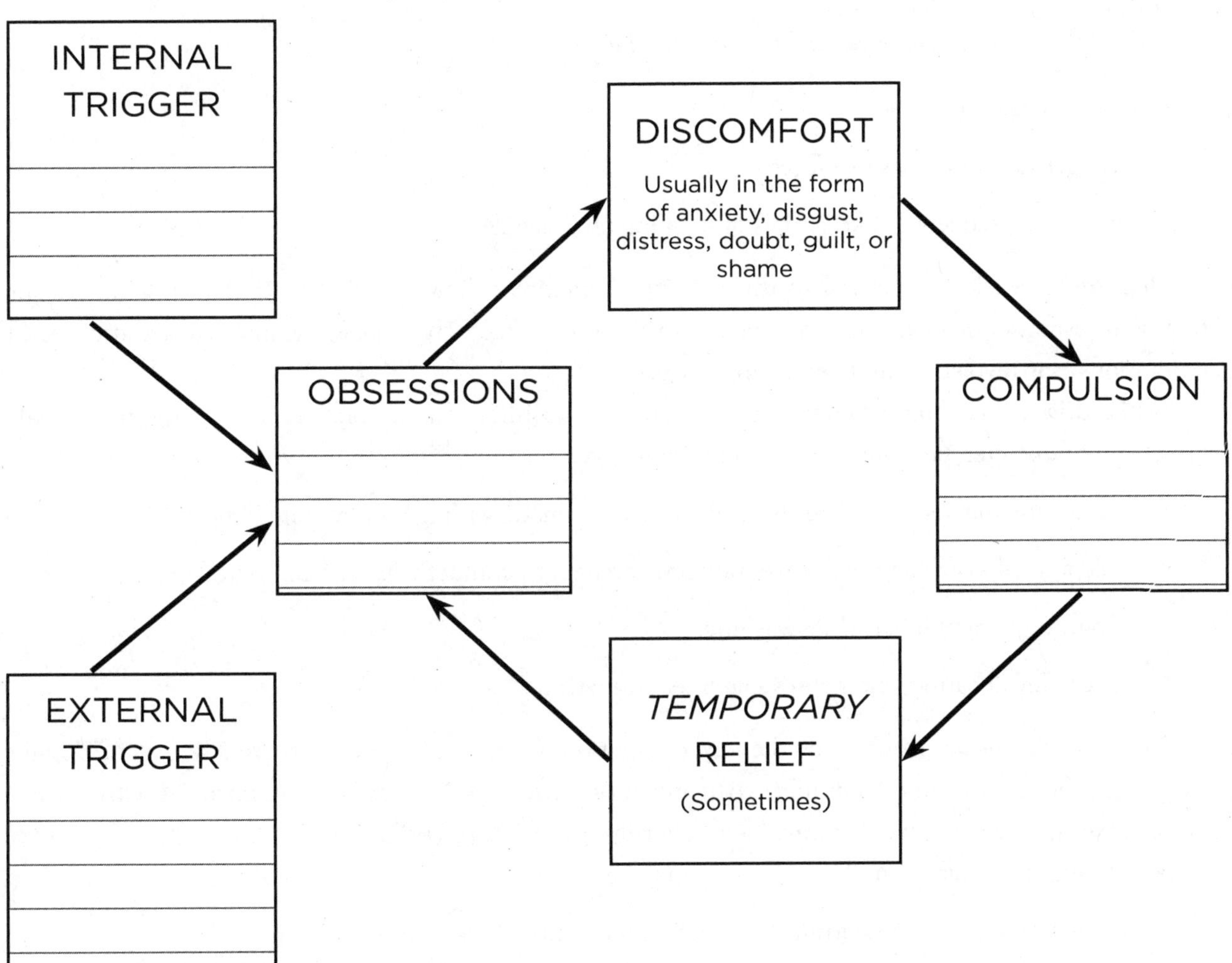

Contamination OCD

Contamination obsessions are among the most commonly depicted manifestations of OCD. Oftentimes, these obsessions center around discomfort about physical contaminants like germs, illness, fecal matter, blood, poison, or chemicals. Places associated with these contaminants, like public restrooms and hospitals, are common triggers, though everyday items, like doorknobs and cellphones, also elicit related distress. Common obsessions include:

Thoughts like:

What if I contract a blood-borne illness and infect my unborn child?

Maybe I didn't wash my hands enough after cleaning the house.

What if this food was poisoned, and I die because I eat it?

Intrusive images of:

- Triggering substances like feces.
- Feared consequences like visuals of stepping on a needle.

Oftentimes, anxiety is central to this subtype. Sometimes, however, disgust is the most significant emotional response for folks with this theme. In these instances, the obsessions may involve urges, and compulsions may revolve around decreasing disgust.

While this theme is most famously associated with washing compulsions and avoidance, individuals with this subtype often perform mental compulsions like:

- Reviewing memories to determine if contact was made with a contaminated object.
- Keeping tabs of what items have indirectly come into contact with contaminated items.
- Counting to a number while washing.
- Internally debating whether it's safe to eat something.

Some individuals are troubled by the idea of emotional contamination. For these folks, it's as though emotional experiences will contaminate their mood or sense of well-being. Items associated with certain emotional events or with specific individuals may trigger these obsessions.

For these individuals, mental compulsions may involve:

- Repeating phrases to neutralize contact with emotional contaminants.
- Tracing an image in their mind's eye to protect them from the emotional contaminant.

OCD Process Statement

______________________ led to ______________________________________.
a triggered occurred — an obsession (intrusive thought, image, urge, emotion, or "What if?"

The obsession made me feel ______________________________________.
an emotion (e.g. amxiety, doubt, distress, guilt, shame, discomfort, disgust)

In response to the thought and feeling, I wanted to ______________________________.
perform a compulsion

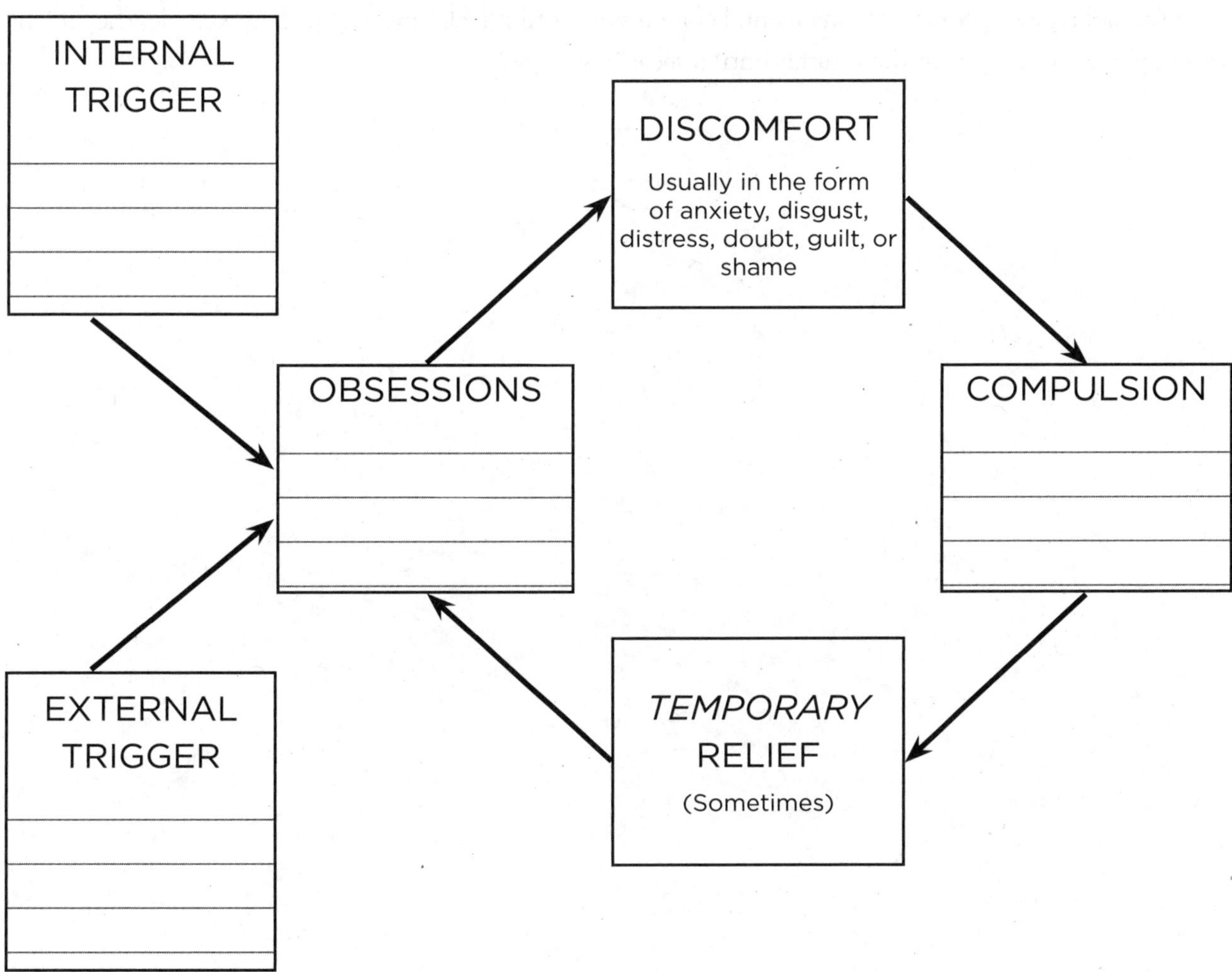

Just Right OCD

"Just right" obsessions usually involve a sense that something is wrong or needs to be fixed. Sometimes, "just right" obsessions are related to another subtype. For instance, someone might think, *If I don't pray until it feels "just right," maybe I'm a bad person and God will never forgive me.* Sometimes the distress itself is the primary driver of compulsions: *If I don't wash my hands until it feels just right then maybe I'll feel uncomfortable forever.* As with disgust-based contamination obsessions, sometimes doubt isn't primary for folks with "just right" obsessions. They may do compulsions with the aim of eliminating discomfort that they simply do not want to feel in the here and now.

Most, if not all, just right obsessions lead to mental compulsions, given that knowing if you feel "just right" necessitates emotional checking. Other mental compulsions might be involved. In fact, someone with this subtype might perform *any* mental compulsion until it feels "just right." For example, they might repeat phrases or prayers in their minds until it feels "just right."

OCD Process Statement

______________ led to ______________.
a triggered occurred — an obsession (intrusive thought, image, urge, emotion, or "What if?"

The obsession made me feel ______________.
an emotion (e.g. amxiety, doubt, distress, guilt, shame, discomfort, disgust)

In response to the thought and feeling, I wanted to ______________.
perform a compulsion

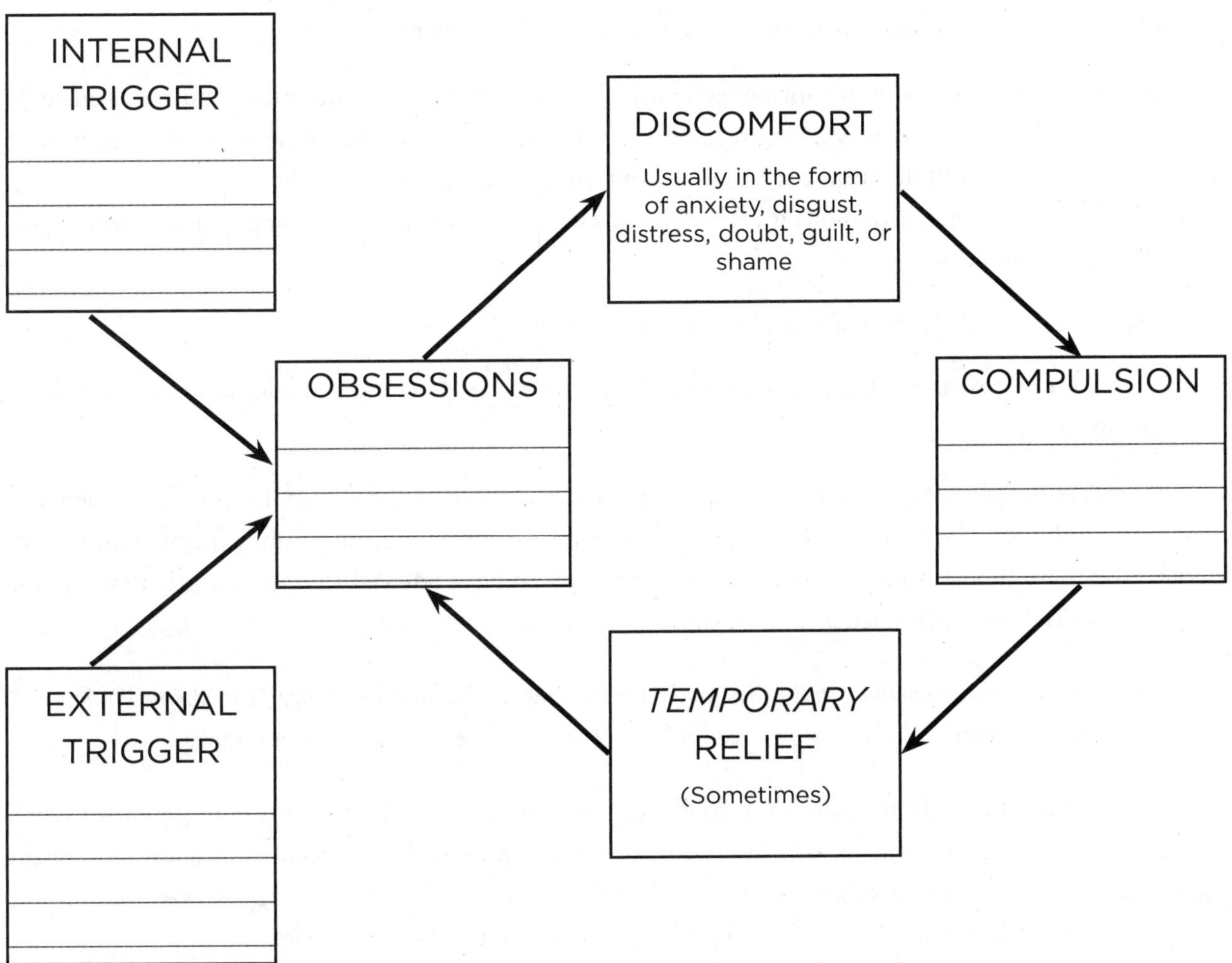

Recovery-Related Obsessions

OCD has a way of folding in on itself and becoming completely disorienting. This is the case with recovery-related obsessions. It's quite common for people in treatment for OCD to experience obsessions about recovery. The anxiety often boils down to concerns about never recovering from OCD. This, of course, makes total sense! People with OCD find themselves sacrificing their lives to the disorder. The idea that one might not recover is scary! Obsessions related to this core concern can sound like:

What if I always have obsessions and they ruin my life?

Maybe I'm unknowingly doing compulsions *and will never recover!*

If I don't do therapy perfectly then I'm doomed to suffer for the rest of my days!

This concern about doing therapy perfectly usually arises when people are trying to use treatment to get rid of thoughts and feelings. Viewing recovery as a practice aimed at improving your relationship with thoughts and feelings will diminish the likelihood of trying to do therapy perfectly.

Some recovery-related obsessions involve concerns that anxiety is legitimate and requires more attention. This can sound like:

What if I don't really have OCD, and I'm just lying to myself?

What if my obsessions are accurate reflections of my character and, by doing treatment, the outcome I fear comes to pass?

Recovery-related obsessions are generally secondary to another subtype of OCD. Say that someone is diagnosed with OCD because they have intrusive thoughts about murdering a family member and doubt about what these thoughts mean. They may begin therapy and feel relieved to know that there is a name for what they've been experiencing. Then a thought might occur to them:

Maybe I didn't share something that would make my therapist realize that I'm dangerous! Maybe I'm just trying to con everyone into believing I have OCD so that I can give in to my murderous urges.

Even when we highlight the element of doubt and the excessive, unhelpful nature of responding to such thoughts, people still feel anxious about the possibility that they could have been misdiagnosed or might never recover. While these possibilities may be remote, they exist and thus are fodder for obsessions.

Mental compulsions aimed at addressing anxieties within this subtype include:

- Reassuring oneself that they are doing exposure work correctly.
- Ruminating about whether a thought is "an OCD thought" or a "real thought."
- Excessively analyzing whether a behavior is compulsive.

It is crucial to understand how to approach recovery effectively. It's also beyond understandable that a person would want clarity about their diagnosis. These desires only become a part of the disorder when people respond to them excessively. The goal here is not to pathologize a desire to learn but rather to recognize how tricky OCD is and ultimately help you along the road to wellness.

OCD Process Statement

____________________ led to ____________________________________.
a triggered occurred — an obsession (intrusive thought, image, urge, emotion, or "What if?"

The obsession made me feel ____________________________________.
an emotion (e.g. amxiety, doubt, distress, guilt, shame, discomfort, disgust)

In response to the thought and feeling, I wanted to __________________________.
perform a compulsion

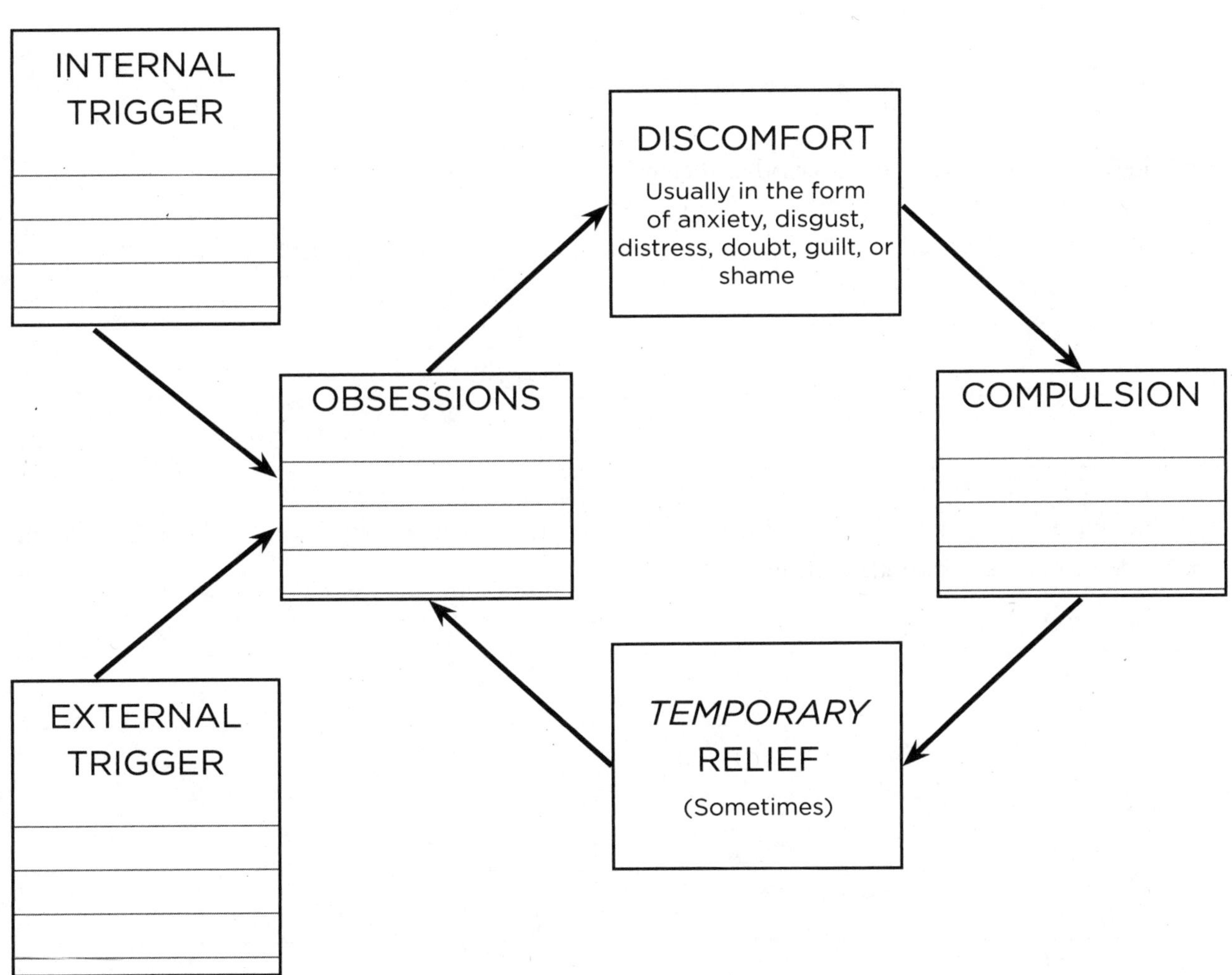

Your Experience and Subtypes

Now that you've read through some of the most common subtypes, take a moment to reflect on your own experience. What themes do you most relate to?

Do you see the element of doubt at play in your experience?

How does your experience differ from other themes?

Are the differences you noted between themes related to the content? If so, can you see how the differing *content* doesn't change the underlying *process*?

As a reminder: the subtypes listed here aren't exhaustive. Subtypes are simply observed trends in people's obsessions. The lines between different categories are arbitrary and often blur together. For instance, someone might be concerned that they have schizophrenia—a mental health obsession—but they might fear "losing their minds" specifically because they could "snap" and become a danger to others. Is this harm OCD or mental health OCD? It could be categorized as either or both, and, ultimately, it doesn't matter. What matters is the intolerance of and efforts to resolve distress or doubt.

How People Get Stuck

People with OCD are chasing temporary relief through mental compulsions. To give you a clearer picture of how temporary relief comes up in your own obsessive-compulsive cycle, consider the process statement placed throughout this chapter from a slightly different angle. Notice that I've added another sentence to the end of the process statement:

> OCD Process Statement
>
> ______________ led to ______________.
> (a triggered occurred) (an obsession (intrusive thought, image, urge, emotion, or "What if?")
>
> The obsession made me feel ______________.
> (an emotion (e.g. amxiety, doubt, distress, guilt, shame, discomfort, disgust))
>
> In response to the thought and feeling, I wanted to ______________.
> (perform a compulsion)
>
> I wanted to do this in order to ______________.
> (neutralize a threat or emotion)

That "in order to" could involve knowing that you're a good person. It could involve getting rid of an image. It might be focused on getting rid of doubt that you're in the "wrong" relationship, the worry you'll lose your mind, or the thought that you'll murder someone. Ultimately, we can boil the "in order to" down further: People do compulsions to get rid of internal experiences—thoughts, feelings, urges, and sensations—that they don't like. Chapter 3 will discuss internal experiences in a little more detail.

Chapter 3

Internal Experiences

Before we proceed with how you can support yourself in navigating thoughts, feelings, urges, and sensations, it's important that we clarify what these experiences involve. Maybe this sounds overly simple, but you wouldn't believe how many misconceptions exist about what thoughts, feelings, urges, and sensations *actually* are.

The thing is, words can mean different things and, as a result, meaning can get lost in translation. Order chips at an English pub and you'll get the equivalent of french fries from an American diner. Ask for a biscuit over high tea in the UK, and you'll get the cookie you might order from a bakery in the US.

Even words that we take for granted can mean different things to different people. Of course, it's not such a big deal to get french fries after ordering potato chips. But when we're talking about your mental health, a misunderstanding in meaning could lead you down a time-consuming and detrimental path. That's why this chapter exists.

What's a Thought?

Macmillan Dictionary defines thought as a word, idea, or image that comes into your mind. So, a thought is an internal experience that is often verbal. You might consider thoughts as short stories that your brain tells you, one sentence at a time.

Words and images are constantly coming up in our minds. They can be mundane, like *I need to make my bed.* They can be creative, like *I wonder what the world would be like if everyone walked on their hands.* They can also elicit fear, like *What if I make the wrong choice by turning left and end up getting into a car accident?* Indeed, as we know, obsessions often involve thoughts.

Thoughts are not inherently meaningful. They can be connected or unrelated to reality. I can have the thought *I have brown eyes* even though my eyes are blue. Meanwhile, the thought *I am about 5'7" tall* would be consistent with reality.

We'll be spending a lot of time talking about thoughts. The main point is that they are words or visuals that aren't necessarily reliable and sometimes aren't even particularly interesting.

Identifying Thoughts

Notice what happens after you read each of the prompts in the provided list. You are likely to notice words and images appearing in your mind. When you do, practice witnessing thoughts as they occur in real time. Ultimately, this skill will be important as we go about the task of identifying obsessions:

When I say black, you say ___________________

When I say wrong, you say ___________________

When I say up, you say ___________________

"If you're happy and you know it…" ___________________

Chances are that when I said black, you said white, and when I said wrong, you said right. But this exercise isn't about the specific content of your thoughts. Instead, the aim here is to help you notice words appearing in your mind. Again, watch what thoughts occur when you read the following:

What did you have for lunch yesterday?

How many siblings do you have?

You might notice automatic thoughts here. You might also notice some active thinking as you search your memory. Witnessing thoughts is the first step in responding to them more effectively. As you go about your day, pause from time to time and practice considering what thoughts are arising.

What's a Sensation?

Sensations are the feelings we experience physically in our bodies. You may feel an itch on the bottom of your foot or pressure on your shoulders. These are both examples of sensations.

Many people with OCD find certain sensations triggering. For instance, people with POCD find sensations in their groins trigger thoughts about attraction. The awareness of physical sensations can also be a trigger in hyper-awareness OCD. Someone with this subtype might notice their breathing, then become anxious that they'll always focus on their breath.

When describing a sensation, watch out for the word "like." The phrase "it feels like" describes a cognitive *interpretation* of a physical sensation. If you say, "It feels like I can't breathe," that's an interpretation, usually of the physical sensation of tightness in the chest or throat. Why does this matter? Well, the thought *It feels like I can't breathe* is a lot scarier than My *chest feels tight*. Separating any judgment of feelings from actual sensation stops us from unnecessarily increasing our own distress.

What's an Emotion?

You may be surprised to find that emotions can be quite tricky to pinpoint. Indeed, most people confuse feelings with thoughts and thinking. But emotions aren't verbal experiences at all. As the term "feeling" suggests, they are *felt* experiences. According to neurologist Antonio R. Damasio, "emotions are more or less the complex reactions the body has to certain stimuli." (Lenzen 2005) While Damasio highlights differences between emotions and feelings—with emotions being the raw physical experience and feelings being the mental interpretation of these physical experiences—I'll be using them interchangeably here. After all, when we break down feelings, stripping away the cognitive interpretation, their component parts are emotions and thus physical sensations.

It's a lot easier to accept a concrete physical sensation than it is to accept an abstract experience like "sadness." If I suggest that you accept sadness, you might wonder, *How do I do that?*" Accepting the presence of a heaviness in your chest, a pit in your stomach, or a lump in your throat is more tangible.

While there are several prominent theories about basic human emotions, for simplicity's sake, let's say there are six basic emotions that people experience: happiness, sadness, fear, anger, disgust, and surprise (Ekman 1992). There are lots of variations on these six basic emotions. If you're not sure whether something is a feeling, consider that emotions are typically one word.

Feeling Your Feelings

Let's take a moment to consider what you feel in your body when experiencing distress. To do that, you'll need to feel distress. That wasn't a typo. We want to make you feel distress on purpose so that you can get better at navigating these feelings.

Let's start with something that makes you *slightly* uncomfortable. Think of something that is wholly unrelated to your obsessions or any other anxiety disorder. Maybe the idea of heights gets you nervous. Maybe the idea of having a sticky residue on your fingers brings about disgust. If we're putting discomfort on a 0–10 scale with 0 being no discomfort and 10 being the most discomfort, we're aiming for a 3 or 4.

Once you have the trigger in mind, imagine the last time you encountered the trigger. For example, when did you last go to a high place? Set a timer for thirty seconds and close your eyes. Then try to recall the details of this experience. For height-related anxiety, you might think back to the view from the top of a tall building. Remember the rushing sensation as the elevator climbed upward and the trees grew smaller.

Once the timer goes off, you may feel a little tense. Great! This is exactly what we need. Now scan through your body. Starting at the top of your head, slowly move downward across your forehead, eyes, nose, cheeks, lips, tongue, jaw, and throat. Notice your neck, shoulders, chest, back, and stomach. Anything in your gut? Your extremities? Make note of what's coming up, one body part at a time. Do you feel any tightness? How about movement or pressure?

The experience may be quite subtle. That's okay. Remember, we weren't shooting for intense. Just notice whatever is there, even if it's not out of the ordinary.

Allowing for these experiences to be present is the essence of *feeling* a feeling. You don't need to do anything special with the physical experiences. In future chapters, we'll discuss mindfulness practices you can use to support you in accepting your emotions. In the meantime, consider that it's no more complicated than bearing witness to sensory experiences in your body.

Why Understanding Emotions Matters

If accepting a feeling is so simple, why is it important to talk about it in such detail? As I mentioned, people often confuse feeling with thoughts and thinking. This can lead to a few different problems.

Confusing Thinking for Feeling

People often confuse thinking and feeling. As a result, they might think about their emotions when someone suggests they allow themselves to feel.

Why is this a problem? Imagine for a moment that you are feeling sad. The emotion involves physical sensations in the body—perhaps a heaviness in your chest or a lump in your throat. On the other hand, *thinking* about sadness involves talking to yourself. This internal discussion may be about why you're sad, what it means that you're sad, or how unfair it is that you're sad. Acknowledging the lump in your throat is very different from thinking about how much better your life would be if you didn't have a feeling. As you can see, thinking and feeling are two different processes.

How might people mistake thinking for feeling in OCD? Let's imagine I have self-harm OCD, and I'm trying to accept my feelings. If I confuse feeling an emotion with thinking about an emotion, I may end up analyzing why I'm anxious and what this means about my safety rather than noticing the physical sensations that comprise anxiety. In essence, I'll do a compulsion instead of feeling an emotion.

Thinking about a feeling is likely to increase that emotion. Trying to resolve why I'm feeling anxious is unlikely to lead me to a definitive conclusion. Because of this, I'll probably feel anxious about my inability to resolve anxiety. I'll probably find that there are a lot of reasons I could be feeling anxious, which may lead me to experience frustration and confusion. And if I'm thinking about how anxious I am and how much I dislike feeling anxious, I'm probably going to feel sadness.

You get the idea. If we try to feel an emotion and instead engage in thinking about an emotional experience, then we will likely increase the emotion itself and create additional emotions.

Are You Thinking or Feeling?

Use the examples in the previous section and in the grid to consider the difference between thinking about and feeling *your* emotions.

Remember: thinking about your feelings involves telling a story about your feelings, whereas feeling an emotion involves identifying and making space for the related physical sensations.

Thinking about an emotion	Feeling an emotion
I'm so sad! I can't believe they said that about me. I thought they were my friends. I guess they don't really care about me at all.	*I'm noticing a sinking feeling in my chest. My jaw is lax and there's a hollowness in my stomach. My muscles are heavy.*

So, emotions aren't always what they might initially appear to be. Hopefully you can see how experiencing an emotion is different from thinking about and analyzing emotional experiences. Properly identifying feelings is a key part of accepting them. After all, if we don't know what we're accepting, we may try to accept feelings and end up thinking about and intensifying our feelings.

Mistaking Having Thoughts for Feelings

It's not just thinking and feeling that get confused. Many mistake passive thoughts for emotions. If, for instance, you have the thought *I feel like I can't do that*, the words "feel like" might lead you to confuse your thought for a feeling. But "can't do that" isn't a feeling. They are words in your mind, which makes them a thought.

If you mistake this thought for a feeling because of the phrase "feels like," you might conclude that accepting your feeling means accepting you "can't do that." Taking the thought at face value rather than accepting the *presence* of the thought and feeling makes it more likely that you'll engage in self-defeating behaviors. In this example, if you accept that you "can't do that," you will probably avoid taking action.

If you, instead, recognize the presence of the thought and the feeling of discouragement that accompanies this thought, you're better able to accept the presence of both thoughts and feelings while you continue to take action. By correctly labeling thoughts and feelings, you have more control over how you behave.

Let's consider another example. You might have the thought *I feel like they're upset with me.* While you likely have an emotion related to the idea that someone is upset with you, the experience described here is actually a thought. If you "feel like they're upset with" you, you're probably having a thought that someone might be upset with you and feelings of sadness related to this thought. If you think you have to accept "they're upset with you" in order to accept the feeling, then you'll probably feel sadder.

Translating "It feels like..."

Take a moment to consider if the phrase "It feels like..." or "I feel like..." comes up when you're talking or thinking about your obsessions. If you immediately have a sense of how the phrases come up in your mind or in discussion, write your examples in the space provided. Then translate this "feels like" into its component parts: the thought and the feeling.

If you're not sure that you use the phrase "It feels like," consider some of the common ways this comes up within OCD:

- *I feel like my thought is true.*
- *I feel like I have to figure this out.*
- *I feel like it's irresponsible to accept doubt.*
- *I feel like I'm a bad person.*

And if none of these examples fit, that's okay! Flag this page or download a copy from http://www.newharbinger.com/55541 and keep your eyes peeled for the phrases "It feels like" or "I feel like." When you notice them, return to this exercise.

"Feels like"	Translation into thoughts and feelings
I feel like I ran over someone with my car.	*I'm having the thought that I ran over someone with my car and I'm feeling anxious.*

What's an Urge?

Urges are impulses to act that are experienced in the body as physical sensations. For example, if you're angry at someone, you might want to yell at them and experience your urge to yell as a tightening in your chest.

Some people with OCD may *fear* that they are having an urge when they don't actually want to take action. Just because you have a thought and a physical sensation doesn't mean you have the genuine desire to act. I could, for instance, experience a tightening in my chest without having an urge to yell at someone. I could also experience thoughts of yelling at someone and tightness in my chest at the same time without having the urge to yell. But the person with moral scrupulosity who is scared they might involuntarily yell obscenities may worry that thoughts of yelling at someone, accompanied by tightness in the chest, *could* indicate a genuine desire and that such a desire *might* mean something about their character. Here we are back with our old friend, doubt. For this person, the thoughts and physical sensations probably trigger a "what if" like "What if this is an urge and I yell at this person?" This doubt about whether they are experiencing a genuine urge could result in a lot of mental analysis!

Of course, people with OCD experience genuine desires just like everyone else. But even when someone experiences an actual urge, they won't necessarily let that urge dictate how they behave. I know this because I, myself, have refrained from making rude gestures after being cut off on the freeway. We make the choice to tolerate urges all the time for the sake of being the kind of people we want to be.

Recognizing the element of choice with acting out urges is particularly important for those who experience obsessions as urges. Just because I have the urge to rid myself of disgust doesn't mean I have to neutralize disgust by imagining something clean. Just because I have the urge to get rid of discomfort related to things being out of place, doesn't mean that I have to order them symmetrically in my mind. Knowing that these urges don't always require action is key if you're to stop mental compulsions.

Even if you rationally understand that responding to urges is a choice, experiencing an urge can trigger obsessions. Let's say that person with moral scrupulosity actually wanted to yell an obscenity. They might fear that the urge could overcome them or that having the urge makes them a bad person. Thus, the urge triggers what ifs that could easily lead to endless analysis about the quality of one's character.

By noticing experiences nonjudgmentally—whether these experiences involve genuine urges or intrusive "urges"—we can notice thoughts about whether something is an urge without evaluating if we are experiencing *genuine* urges or if we might want to act on the urges. This sets the stage for dropping mental compulsions.

Putting It Into Practice

As you're continuing about your daily life, here are a few tidbits to keep in mind:

- Thoughts are words or images in your mind.
- Sensations are physical feelings in the body.
- Feelings or emotions are a group of physical sensations in your body.
- Thinking about a feeling is different from feeling a feeling.
- If you say, "It feels like," you're talking about a thought rather than a feeling.
- Urges are desires that are also experienced physically.
- Physical sensations and thoughts are not always indicative of genuine desires.

Now that you have a more in-depth understanding of these internal experiences, we can talk about how to navigate them more effectively. But before we explore specific strategies, we need to decide upon a goal. The next chapter will establish where we're going and why we're going in that direction, so we know how the skills discussed in this book are intended to support us.

Part II

The Villain

Now that we know what we're working with, we need to establish what we're working toward. Getting on the same page about what the problems and solutions are can mean the difference between building recovery and continuing to suffer. This next chapter will outline why mental compulsions are the problem so that we're clear on why we'd commit to the challenging work that recovery requires.

What hero would strike out on a quest to defeat a villain without understanding who the villain is and why it's important to defeat the villain? So let's discuss our villain: mental compulsions.

Chapter 4

The Fallout of Mental Compulsions

What puts the "disorder" in obsessive-compulsive disorder? We need to grasp what's causing your problems so that we can address what's not working in your life. Might obsessions be the culprit? Actually, research shows that the vast majority of people experience unwanted thoughts, even though only a fraction of individuals struggle with OCD (Bouvard et al. 2017). So **anyone** might experience the intrusive thought *What if I turn my steering wheel and fly off of this overpass?* If people without OCD experience obsessions, then obsessions can't be the issue.

If obsessions aren't universally problematic, what is the difference between those who experience OCD and those who don't? There are likely differences in the frequency of thoughts, images, and urges or in the intensity of emotions people experience secondary to obsessions. Of course, much has already been said about our inability to control what thoughts, images, and urges appear in our minds. But when it comes to internal experiences, obsessions aren't the only thing beyond our control. As it turns out, we don't have ultimate control over what emotions we experience either.

This leaves one difference between people with and without OCD: how they *respond* to intrusive thoughts. If you do nothing in the face of obsessions, they will naturally come and go. If you try to get rid of obsessions and related emotions, however, then your unwillingness to have these experiences will lead you to do compulsions.

Compulsions aim to control thoughts and feelings. Unfortunately, since we can't control whether obsessions enter our minds or feelings arise, compulsions take control over our lives. Compulsions—including mental compulsions—tend to cause "clinically significant distress or impairment." Translation? Mental compulsions cause issues for people who perform them.

How do mental compulsions cause distress or impairment? Well, whether you're repeating a prayer, lost in a mental argument, or analyzing an experience to try to get an answer, chances are that this will detract from your ability to engage with things that matter to you. Maybe you want to be more connected in conversations. Maybe you simply want to focus more completely on the movie you're watching or the podcast you're listening to. Either way, mental compulsions rob you of time and stand between you and the life you want to live.

Given this, treatment for OCD addresses the "distress and impairment" by teaching people to stop performing compulsions.

It can be tricky to disengage from invisible behaviors, and scary to let them go. Let's consider the specific problems mental compulsions cause so that we can develop the resolve to drop them. We'll cover the how-to in upcoming chapters.

Mental Compulsions Take You Out of the Present Moment

Mental compulsions have the unique ability to detract from your life even while you are participating in your life. That's because you can perform a mental compulsion while you're engaged in other behaviors.

When you're performing a mental compulsion, you become increasingly distracted and less present with your experience. For example, let's say an individual has the obsession "What if I'm lying to everyone about my sexual identity?" and this doubt causes anxiety. The person may then start reviewing past relationships, checking their feelings, and analyzing the degree of their attraction in order to reassure themselves that they are identifying authentically. Unfortunately, in this process of trying to reassure themselves, they'll become increasingly distracted from whatever they were doing before the obsession arose. As they scan through their minds, they might, for instance, miss out on part of a lecture or lose time on a test.

By pulling individuals away from the present, mental compulsions rob them of their lives one moment at a time. Thus, while trying to address uncertainty may seem relatively benign, it is anything but.

You might be thinking, *But obsessions distract me!* And yes, obsessions can absolutely distract people. But remember, whether obsessions show up is outside of our control. Mental compulsions, on the other hand, are what absorb our attention on an *ongoing* basis. Obsessions may entice us into our head, but mental compulsions are what keep us stuck there.

Thankfully, we can choose whether we perpetuate the distraction. Chasing a distraction-free mind by trying to resolve an obsession doesn't work. The better option here involves accepting that you will experience obsessions and choosing to drop the mental compulsions as soon as you catch them.

In chapter 1, you wrote down some examples of the mental compulsions you tend to perform. Reflect on that list for a moment and choose one. Now, consider what you were doing the last time you were performing this mental compulsion. Were you in class? Having dinner with a friend? Write down the activity in the space provided.

____

How did these mental behaviors keep you out of the present moment? If you were analyzing the quality of your relationship, did that interfere with your ability to follow along with a movie? If you were trying to get certainty that you weren't living in a simulation, did that keep you from tracking what the teacher was saying? Use the space to journal about your experience.

Mental Compulsions Can Trigger Obsessions

While mental compulsions are intended to resolve distress, they often *create* more triggers. For example, if you have relationship OCD, you might compulsively compare your current and past relationships to reassure yourself that you're in the "right" relationship. While comparing, you may remember something you liked about your ex and feel more anxious about your current relationship. Thus, by actively engaging with compulsions, you've retriggered yourself, creating a new obsession.

Consider some recent instances in which you tried to resolve your obsession. Can you remember retriggering yourself and creating more distress at any point in this process? Maybe you were reminding yourself how much you love your family to reassure yourself that you couldn't kill them, when you remembered feeling angry with your mother. Maybe you were analyzing the nature of reality when you felt a sense of discomfort and wondered, *Is that a sign that I'm not real?*

Journal about your experience:

Mental Compulsions Can Perpetuate Emotional States

In her book *My Stroke of Insight*, neuroanatomist Jill Bolte Taylor explains that once the chemical experience behind emotions is triggered in your body, these chemicals run their course within ninety seconds (Taylor 2008). If we were to visualize this idea, emotions would look like this:

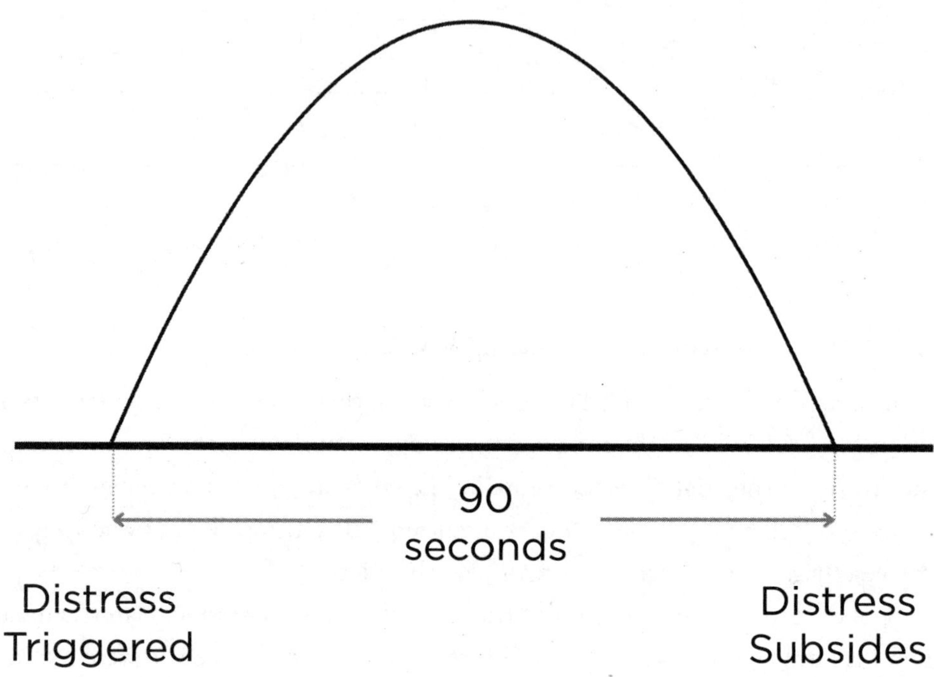

When I share this fact with people, they are often skeptical, given that they've had emotional experiences that last much longer than ninety seconds. How do we reconcile this? Well, the ninety-second chemical cascade can be retriggered. So, if you were being stalked by a tiger, you'd wisely choose to remain on guard and keep thinking about the tiger in the service of your safety. Purposefully thinking about the tiger will perpetuate fear.

Likewise, when you perceive that an emotion is lasting longer than ninety seconds, active thinking is probably keeping your emotions alive. Mental compulsions are one such type of thinking. Let's consider the trajectory of feelings in the context of OCD. If you accept your feelings and drop thinking, your emotions would initially surge and then settle, reducing the mental compulsions' interference with your life in the meantime.

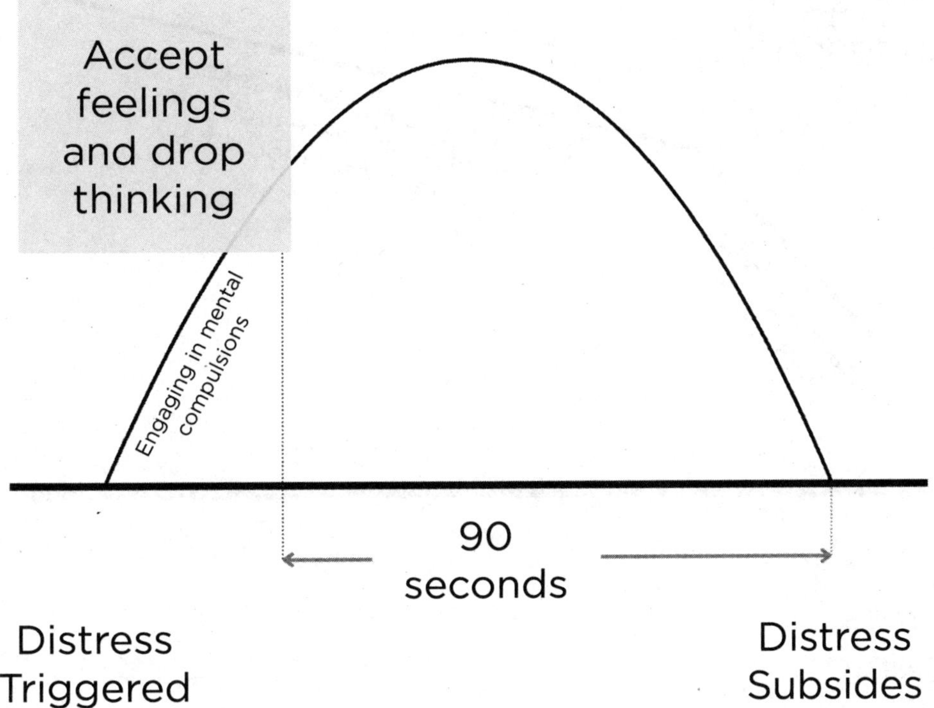

When you continue engaging with an obsession by performing mental compulsions, you are reigniting and prolonging the emotional response to that obsession. In this way, the mental compulsions that are intended to resolve feelings actually perpetuate our emotional responses.

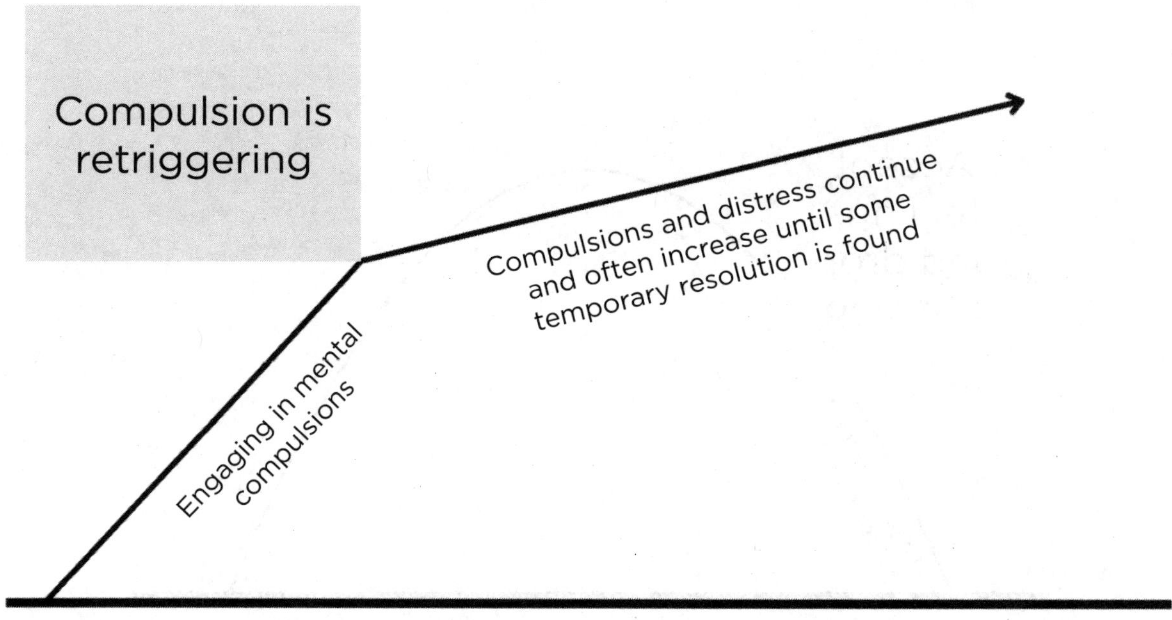

So, we can let emotions wash over us or keep them alive through active thinking. Given that emotions naturally subside on their own, in a minute and a half, no less, it doesn't make sense to try to eradicate them. Embracing that ninety-second chemical reaction by accepting the presence of your feelings seems well worth it if it helps you get your life back!

Consider for a moment what difficult things you've been able to do for ninety seconds at a time. Have you engaged in intense exercise in short spurts? Have you experienced contractions while giving birth? Maybe you've endured a brief, uncomfortable medical procedure?

____

____

____

If you could live through these experiences, do you think you might be able to accept discomfort ninety seconds at a time?

Mental Compulsions → More Mental Compulsions

Every time a mental compulsion alleviates your distress temporarily, you make it more likely that you will perform a mental compulsion again. Why? Well, using technical jargon, the answer is negative reinforcement (Skinner 1976).

Let's break down these two words: "negative" and "reinforcement." Suppose I have a headache. Most people can agree that this is an unpleasant experience. In response to the headache, I might decide to take a painkiller. If that painkiller reduces or gets rid of the headache, then I will be more likely to take a painkiller the next time I have a headache. This is negative reinforcement:

> Getting rid of something, like a headache, is the "negative" part. Think of it as subtracting from the experience.
>
> The "reinforcement" part references the behaviors that are more likely to be repeated to reduce unpleasant experiences—like taking ibuprofen.

Now imagine you have the thought *What if I'm a bad person?* and you find yourself reviewing your memories to reassure yourself that you've done good things and thus cannot be "bad." If you successfully convince yourself that you're not "bad," then this mental reassurance is negatively reinforced.

Unfortunately, negative reinforcement doesn't consider that compulsive behaviors aren't in your long-term interest. If the mental compulsion alleviates pain, you'll be compelled to do it again even if it causes more harm overall, just as some continue to take ibuprofen for headaches even after experiencing stomach problems. Negative reinforcement makes you a slave to behaviors even though they (1) don't always work and (2) detract from life.

Consider how your mental compulsions sometimes provide relief. If you have harm OCD, does avoiding crime shows reduce anxiety? If you have sexual orientation OCD, does checking your feelings sometimes lead to confidence in your attraction and decrease fear? Write an example in the space provided.

____

____

____

____

In your example, what is the occasional relief, and how does it drive continued mental compulsions? Jot this down.

____

____

Mental Compulsions Make You Dependent on Mental Compulsions

We learn through bearing witness to our own behaviors. As Jon Hershfield writes in *When A Family Member has OCD*, "Once the brain witnesses the feared situation without the compulsive response, it has to recalculate its position that the feared situation always warrants a compulsive response" (Hershfield 2015, 66–67).

Unfortunately, the reverse is also true. When your brain witnesses you engaging in a compulsive behavior secondary to anxiety or distress, it learns that the behavior is keeping you safe or is required to handle emotions, which makes you dependent on compulsions.

This reminds me of a story:

> A man living in New Jersey sits on his porch day after day with a shotgun in hand. He practically lives on this porch. Frankly, it worries some of his neighbors. One day, although it seems like a risky move, a passerby approaches the man and says, "Hey, why do you sit on your porch with that shotgun all day?" The man says without hesitation, "To keep the lions away, of course." The passerby pauses, puzzled. "What lions?" he asks. The man replies: "Exactly! You don't see any lions *because* I guard the neighborhood so well."

Just like the man from New Jersey, you could choose to continue engaging in compulsions and reinforce the importance of performing them. The trouble is, when you always do compulsions, you never learn that you might not *need* to do them. You can teach yourself that you are capable of living with distress by dropping compulsions. This has the potential to set you free.

Mental Compulsions Become Harder to Resist

In his book *The Upward Spiral*, Alex Korb talks about the neural underpinnings of decision-making. In simple terms, he discusses three parts of the brain involved in decision-making: the prefrontal cortex, the dorsal striatum, and the nucleus accumbens. He notes that each of these parts of the brain gets a vote when it comes to decision-making.

The prefrontal cortex tends to vote based on what's rational. The nucleus accumbens, which is involved in addiction, casts its vote based on what will feel best in the moment. The dorsal striatum votes based on what a person has done historically. The more frequently you do something, the more likely your dorsal striatum will vote to do it again.

All of this to say that every time you do mental compulsions, you influence the dorsal striatum's vote, making mental compulsions more challenging to resist.

The good news? Every time that you make the choice to refrain from mental compulsions, you are making it easier to disengage from them in the future.

While this book has yet to cover the "how" of resisting mental compulsions, we know that they are behaviors that we can change. So, let's consider how you've managed to change other behaviors. Think of one instance in which you've changed a behavior. Maybe you started walking regularly or getting to bed earlier. Whatever behavior, no matter how big or small, write it down here.

____

____

Consider what it was like at first. Did you find it difficult to go to bed earlier when the next TV episode began auto playing? Did you struggle to get out of the house for that walk because of other items on your to-do list?

____

____

Now consider how your ability to stick with that behavior evolved with practice. Did it become easier to maintain this habit every time you practiced?

____

____

Do Mental Compulsions Work?

As you can see, mental compulsions carry a hefty price tag and tend to be self-perpetuating. But are they worth the cost? Do they actually work?

The short answer is no, mental compulsions don't work.

Now, this answer does depend on how you define "work." As we've covered, sometimes, you will review, ruminate, analyze, neutralize, or somehow compulse and you will get short-lived relief. But if the goal of mental compulsions is to rid you of obsessions or emotions, or to ensure safety in the face of doubt and fear, then they do not accomplish the job. When compulsions alleviate discomfort, discomfort will invariably resurface given the nature of life.

Certainty Doesn't Exist

What about uncertainty? Adding insult to injury, mental compulsions are not capable of eliminating uncertainty. In fairness, trying to get absolute certainty is *always* a fool's errand because nothing in life is 100 percent certain.

I imagine that you feel confident that the sun will rise tomorrow. I know I do. Thus far, the sun has risen every day of our lives. In theory, though, something could collide with the earth, slowing or stopping its rotation and plunging part of the planet into a state of perpetual night. Thus, while it's exceedingly likely that the sun will rise tomorrow, I cannot be 100 percent sure that it will.

If we cannot have certainty about something you can literally set your clock by, how in the world can we get certainty about what actions you might take in a year or how you might feel next week? Will you still feel attracted to the same person? Will you harm someone? Will you experience psychosis? Who knows! We cannot even know for a fact that we're alive or that we're not living in a simulation.

We can feel more or less confident in the face of doubt. But here's the thing: we can't control confidence because confidence is a feeling. Besides, confidence doesn't necessarily have any bearing on certainty. People can be simultaneously very confident and hopelessly ignorant about the same thing. In fact, oftentimes people who are less informed have a greater sense of confidence. (To learn more, look up the Dunning-Kruger effect.) And while people with OCD centering on doubt are seeking confidence, this confidence doesn't afford protection from disaster.

Confidence can be particularly elusive when it comes to inherently ambiguous questions. For instance, someone with sexual orientation OCD might have the thought *What if I'm secretly gay?* Given that sexual orientation exists on a spectrum and can be a moving target, it's not possible for one to definitively pinpoint where on the spectrum they exist. Besides, to get certainty about one's sexual orientation, we would have to:

1. quantify exactly what attraction is,
2. find a way to objectively measure attraction, and
3. determine what degree of attraction a person has to feel toward how many individuals to be classified as a certain orientation.

There are just over eight billion people on this planet and, therefore, a whole lot of opinions and possible criteria.

Let's walk through one more hypothetical. A person with relationship OCD might worry, *What if my partner isn't the best fit for me?* Getting certainty about this is, once again, a lost cause. Why? Well, trying to answer whether someone is the best fit for you begs the question: What makes someone a "good" fit for another person? Should someone who is a "good fit" never challenge their partner or cause them discomfort? Should they be similar or dissimilar to their partner and to what extent? If we decided what the criteria were, could there be someone out there who is better for you? In theory. But it would take many, many, many lifetimes to meet with every potential partner and to compare all potential partners to each other. It's simply not reasonable.

Given that compulsions cannot offer you absolute certainty, they cannot actually prevent feared outcomes from occurring, either. You could have a sense of confidence that you're in the "right" relationship and still get divorced. You could have a sense of confidence about your sexual orientation and later determine that you're attracted to someone who doesn't fit the parameters of your "type." No matter how many times you review the contents of your inner world, you won't prevent outcomes that you don't want. You could say a prayer five times when you have thoughts regarding your family's safety and your family could still be harmed.

Understanding that certainty doesn't exist helps to motivate us to take the steps necessary to recover.

Can You Attain Certainty?

If your compulsions are aimed at finding certainty, consider if certainty is even attainable. If you have harm OCD, can you prove that you won't harm someone? If you have neutral obsessions, can you prove with certainty that your awareness won't drive you mad? Is it possible to eliminate all the possibilities you don't want? What stands in the way of absolute certainty?

____

____

____

____

Might you be seeking confidence rather than absolute certainty? Write down your thoughts in the space provided.

____

____

____

____

And if getting certainty isn't possible, is it worth giving up so much in pursuit of confidence, which cannot prevent dreaded outcomes?

____

____

____

Empowering You to Drop Mental Compulsions

Since we cannot control the presence of obsessions, and we can't make ourselves feel an emotion, responding differently to these experiences is the only viable path to recovery. Now that you understand the active component of thinking, you have the power to navigate the experience differently. What does responding differently look like? In short, it involves dropping mental compulsions once you recognize that you're engaged in them.

I want to take a moment here to acknowledge that the idea of giving up mental compulsions may sound really scary! Refraining from excessive washing is scary for the person with contamination OCD even if they understand rationally that the amount of washing is probably unnecessary. Likewise, refraining from analysis is scary for a person who understands that excessive thinking probably isn't the answer.

Remember, though, no matter how much you wash, uncertainty about whether your hands are dirty will exist. The same is true for mental compulsions: no matter how much you ruminate, you still won't be certain you aren't missing a critical piece of information. And no matter how many times you neutralize a disgust-provoking thought with a more pleasant one, you will experience more disgust again at some point. The promise of mental compulsions is "If you think just a little bit more, then it will resolve the discomfort you feel." This is a hollow promise. **Mental compulsions are the problem masquerading as the solution.** They interfere with your ability to be present, distract from important conversations, interfere with moments of connection, and isolate you in the process. They take up time that might otherwise be spent on creative hobbies or meaningful work. They create more distress and perpetuate existing distress. They make you increasingly reliant on mental compulsions, and they don't even deliver on the promise of lasting comfort or certainty. If mental compulsions don't work, then they aren't worth the sacrifices they demand!

When we can accept the fact that triggers happen and obsessions arise, we can prioritize what matters most to us. **If mental compulsions have gotten you further and further from the life that you want, learning how to behave differently is the key to turning things around and building that life!**

Part III

The Heroes of Our Story

Now that we know the differences between obsessions and mental compulsions, and why we want to stop mental compulsions, we can explore how to accept obsessions and emotions and disengage from active thinking. To support you with this, we'll be talking about cognitive behavioral therapy (CBT). This approach involves better understanding your thoughts, feelings, and behaviors as well as how they influence each other. With OCD treatment, we emphasize the B in CBT using an approach known as exposure and response prevention (ERP). This involves gradually facing triggers so you learn to experience triggers without performing compulsions. CBT and ERP have demonstrated a high degree of efficacy across extensive studies over decades of research (Reid et al. 2021). As a result, CBT is generally the first-line treatment for OCD. While studies usually emphasize the ERP portion of treatment, there is evidence that the C, or cognitive part of CBT, is also useful in recovery (Ferrando and Selai 2021; Rosa-Alcázar et al. 2008). Thus, current standards suggest the use of both cognitive and behavioral interventions (Van Noppen et al. 2021), and we'll cover both approaches in this book.

We'll also be using acceptance and commitment therapy (ACT), another evidence-based treatment for OCD (Soondrum et al. 2022; Twohig et al. 2024). ACT is part of the "third wave" of behavioral therapies that focus on mindfulness practice. The practice of ERP is just as important within ACT, though the emphasis of ERP is slightly different within the ACT framework. Without getting TOO nerdy or acronym heavy on you, let's discuss how ERP works and why we'll focus on practicing ERP from an ACT perspective.

Traditionally, ERP has emphasized a process called habituation. Simply put, habituation refers to the fact that the distress caused by triggers dissipates over time. When you're repeatedly exposed to a trigger and you don't respond, you eventually get bored of your triggers.

Consider the classic example of Pavlov's dogs (Clark 2004). When regularly fed food after a bell was rung, the dogs learned to associate the bell with food. Thus, they salivated when the bell rang even if no food was present. Once the association between the bell and food had been established, researchers rang the bell repeatedly *without* offering food to the dogs. Over time, the salivation response was "extinguished"; the dogs disassociated the bell from food and no longer salivated after the bell rang.

As Pavlov's dogs associated the bell with food and thus salivated, people with OCD associate certain triggers with threat and feel distress. They might, for instance, associate an image of a car accident with danger and feel anxious. They may then learn to associate activities that bring up this image—like driving or seeing a news story about a car accident—with danger and anxiety, too. And so, many experiences come to trigger anxiety.

If no danger follows a trigger, then we would anticipate the associated emotion would subside just as salivation eventually stopped when food didn't follow the bell. Unfortunately, compulsions complicate matters. When people behave compulsively to alleviate their distress, they reinforce the idea that the trigger signifies a genuine threat and that compulsions are necessary to neutralize that threat. The person in the car might review their memories to determine if a car accident occurred. If nothing happens—police don't show up to arrest them—they learn not that they are safe but that their well-being hinges upon the act of reviewing their memories. Thus, the reviewing behavior is reinforced and interferes with disassociating the trigger and expected danger.

If, however, a person with OCD is presented with a trigger and does nothing to reinforce the belief in perceived threat, they have a chance to disconnect the trigger from the sense of threat. When you don't respond to triggers and catastrophe doesn't follow, the association between triggers and danger subsides. What's more, while distress will spike at first, it will naturally dissipate over time since that's what feelings do. And with each exposure to the trigger, people become less sensitive to the trigger just as Pavlov's dogs became less sensitive to the bell. This will ultimately lead them to disassociate the distress from the trigger.

If a person with hit-and-run OCD did ERP, they would repeatedly drive, watch the news, and invoke those images of accidents while refraining from mentally reviewing. From a habituation point of view, their anxiety would dissipate over time—both during exposure and between exposures. In this process, the link between the triggers and fear would go away.

Habituation does tend to happen, but it doesn't always. Feelings are fickle, and depending on them to behave reliably isn't reasonable. That said, changing your feelings isn't necessary. In fact, studies have found that habituation is a poor predictor of long-term recovery (Craske et al. 2014). Thus, as time has gone on, other theories of and approaches to ERP have emerged.

Inhibitory learning theory, for one, views exposure as a means to create new associations that compete with (or inhibit) the older associations over time (Jacoby and Abramowitz 2016). The focus isn't on getting rid of associations but developing additional ones. Translation: If I associate the image of a car accident with the potential for catastrophe occurring and do exposure and response prevention without experiencing catastrophe, then after some time sans catastrophe or compulsions, the association between the image and nothing happening will become stronger. The association with nothing happening will outweigh the association with catastrophe, and I'll learn safety. The new association will inhibit my fear even though the association between the image and the possibility of an accident will never completely disappear. There are lots of other associations that can be overwritten in this process. For instance, if some feared event happens, I'll have the chance to associate the feared outcome with (a) absolute incapacitation or with (b) the ability to cope. B will have the chance to crowd out A. Not only will people come to understand that feared outcomes are less likely and that they are more capable of navigating challenges, they will also have the chance to learn, experientially, that they are capable of being in the presence of their thoughts and feelings.

In this approach, someone with hit-and-run OCD would also drive as exposure and refrain from mentally reviewing as response prevention. The exposures themselves might look a bit different, though, as this approach uses information about optimizing learning to increase the impact of ERP. It encourages people to do multiple exposures at the same time across contexts as research shows this supports learning. It also suggests that we contrast the expected outcome—an inability to cope—and the actual outcome—the ability to handle anxiety—to help us appreciate our own capacity. Inhibitory learning theory is less focused on doing exposures in a gradual, stepwise fashion given that the element of surprise has been found to foster learning. To some degree, decreasing emotions is still a goal within this model, though the framework emphasizes distress tolerance over getting rid of feelings.

ACT takes ERP a step further and suggests that the associated thoughts and feelings are not the problem at all. Instead, it's our *relationship* to thoughts and feelings that causes so much trouble (Harris 2008). When we allow our thoughts and feelings to dictate how we behave, we act in ways that are counter to what matters to us. These actions then interfere with our contentment.

ACT brings two additional focuses to ERP. First, exposures are intended as practices that promote *willingness* to experience thoughts and feelings so that compulsions can't hijack our lives (Twohig et al. 2015). Second, values, the qualities that matter most to us, become the focal point of exposures. The hit-and-run exposure might involve driving to your son's baseball game so that you can be a supportive parent. In this process, you develop willingness to accept thoughts and feelings about the potential for having hit someone so that you can be present to the game.

When considering the evolution of ERP, I often think of a quote by the Buddhist philosopher Shantideva: "How could there be enough leather to cover all the surface of the earth? But with the mere leather of the soles of one's shoes, it's as if all the surface of the earth were covered." Since habituation is not ubiquitous and we cannot exhaust potential causes of anxiety and distress, focusing on reducing the emotions related to all triggers through habituation is akin to trying to cover the earth in leather. Since it's not possible, we will invariably have to avoid some terrain altogether. In this metaphor, ACT is akin to putting on shoes. It gives you the freedom to roam through the world unencumbered by the possible feelings you may encounter.

Bottom line, ERP is considered the gold-standard treatment for OCD with decades of research backing its effectiveness. Response prevention is the most important part of this equation. When you're living with OCD, you are constantly faced with triggers and, as we've been discussing, the compulsions you tend to respond with keep you stuck.

Before you try to enact exposures, we'll be exploring the practice of response prevention. After all, regardless of which approach you ascribe to, doing compulsions makes us reliant on behaviors that interfere with our lives, and response prevention addresses this. Toward this end, we'll cover cognitive strategies, mindfulness, ACT, and some skills from rumination-focused CBT. Once we get a handle on this practice of response prevention, we'll turn our sights toward exposures.

Chapter 5

Cognitive Strategies

Your mind is full of thoughts. In fact, the brain is a remarkable thought-making machine. Research estimates that, on average, people churn out six thousand thoughts per day (Tseng and Poppenk 2020). That's around six-and-a-half thoughts per minute. If I had a dollar for every thought I had, I'd be Scrooge McDuck diving into a swimming pool of cash and so would you.

Even though we have lots of thoughts, most people don't realize that their thoughts are only words in their mind. This is a problem for two reasons: (1) thoughts aren't necessarily factual or important and (2) if we take our thoughts at face value, they become the basis for how we behave.

Cognitive tools are designed to help you consider your thoughts and more deliberately decide if they should inform your actions. Given this, these tools *may* be less relevant for those whose obsessions involve urges to address distress. Such obsessions are more common in presentations of OCD wherein disgust, hyper-awareness, feeling "just right," and achieving symmetry predominate. They may still be of use, though, so I encourage you to read this chapter regardless. If you find that these tools don't apply to you, don't fret. We will cover skills to support acceptance, including acceptance of urges, in the chapters that follow.

Obsessive thoughts can be tricky. Just like junk mail cluttering your inbox, many of the thoughts that pop into your mind—obsessions or otherwise—aren't worth the neurons they rode in on. Unfortunately, we sometimes treat "junk mail," or junk thoughts, as though they were mail marked **URGENT** from a reputable source.

Anyone who has fallen for a phishing scam can relate. You get an email that looks like it's important telling you that you need to "act fast" to avoid some calamity. Before you know it, you've shared personal information with info.afmo239@so-and-so.com. It can be tough to clean up in the aftermath of treating junk mail like it's important.

This is what's happening with thoughts in an OCD sufferer's mind. It's as though your brain can send you messages telling you that you need to do something urgently without having to legitimize its claims. The next thing you know, it has hijacked your behaviors. Your thoughts say *act fast* and they all seem important, so you start doing things you wouldn't otherwise do.

Why Awareness Matters

Imagine that there's a bully following you around. This guy has only unkind things to say and plenty of them. He especially likes to make fun of you, and he calls you an idiot every time you make a mistake. (Rude!)

Now imagine that these unkind words are coming from your own mind. With no external bully to point to, you're likely to assume that all the things being said are facts from some all-knowing narrator. After a while, you'll take the message "mistakes = idiot" to heart and the idea that you're an idiot will be perceived as part of your reality.

As you continue to hear that you're an idiot for making mistakes, this idea will impact your behavior. You'll stop stepping outside of your comfort zone because of the higher likelihood of making mistakes and being bullied. Sadly, by avoiding anything outside of your comfort zone, you will stop growing and you'll miss out on experiences that matter to you.

If, instead, you recognize that it's this bully saying these nasty things, at least you have the awareness that these are *his* words and not necessarily reality. Since you know that what people say is not always true, you would have more objectivity about the messages you're hearing. You probably still won't like hearing that you're an idiot and might worry that the bully is right, but you can be more thoughtful in how you respond to his words.

So it is with thoughts. When you don't see your thoughts as thoughts, they become your reality and you take actions based on that reality. Someone with moral scrupulosity could have the thought *You're immoral.* If this person is unaware that this is a thought, then they're more likely to assume that its content is inherently important and true.

At this point, they may start *responding* to the thought as though it is a significant issue that needs to be addressed. This person might repeatedly review an incident to determine if they acted in a moral way. They might internally debate what makes something moral. One way or another, they might get lost in their own minds trying to address words that are not intrinsically meaningful. Thus, when the thought *I'm immoral* isn't recognized as a thought, it's more likely to lead someone to get stuck in mental compulsions. They could end up spending lots of time trying to resolve something that might not need a resolution.

When you get down to it, the impact of being oblivious to our thoughts is alarming. You may be reacting to a story in your mind as though it were reality. Up until now, you may have trusted your brain absolutely. After all, we are reliant on it in so many ways. Unfortunately, as much as we rely on our minds, its thoughts aren't necessarily trustworthy.

Thoughts: Fact or Fiction?

As we discussed in chapter 3, thoughts are words, images, or ideas that occur in the mind. Just like a book or a movie, these experiences might be total fiction, based on a true story, or entirely factual. It's frustrating to think that your brain might feed you misinformation. You might wonder if your brain is a bully for churning out unreliable thoughts. But before you demonize your brain, please understand that it's not out to get you. It's just *limited*.

You see, our minds' errors in judgment are side effects of mental shortcuts intended to keep us safe and make our lives more streamlined and efficient. Since we don't have time to give deep thought to every choice we make, these shortcuts are important. They ensure that when we have to make split-second decisions, we err on the side of caution.

While these shortcuts are necessary, they come at a cost: the system was designed to make sure we stay alive and not to ensure our happiness. Our brains evolved to keep us from, for example, getting bitten by a snake. Our survival doesn't rely on accurately telling the difference between snakes and sticks; it relies on us guessing snake whenever there's any ambiguity. And so, while efficient and protective, these snap judgments are often inaccurate.

When it comes to brains, there are a lot of problems with the machinery. Keep in mind, though, that any machinery has its glitches. You wouldn't abandon your smartphone just because of a few technical hiccups. You might yell at it, but it remains useful despite momentary annoyances. This is true of the brain as well. While it's imperfect, we don't need to throw the baby out with the bathwater. Your brain is remarkable. We just need to learn its flaws so that we can effectively navigate the information it delivers.

So how do we do this? Well, the errors that our brain makes are *systematic*; they follow certain patterns that make them easier to categorize and identify. When we can learn to spot these patterns, we can consciously consider if our brain's initial assessments should make our choices for us.

Your Brain's Systematic Errors

So how do we recognize our brain's errors? We actually have names for them! As we get to know these thought errors, also known as cognitive distortions (Beck 2011), we can more readily recognize when our thoughts are a little suspicious.

We can view cognitive distortions as ways in which our thoughts distort reality. Ever been to a fun house at a carnival? A strange name, really, as they're usually more creepy than fun. One of the creepiest elements of a funhouse are those strange mirrors. You look in one and suddenly you're a little teapot, short and stout. You look in the next and you're Gumby. Our images get distorted in these mirrors.

Don't believe that your brain could be quite so faulty? Let's do a little experiment to demonstrate.

I Can't Believe My Eyes

Most of us trust our vision. If we see something, we're inclined to feel confident about the existence of that thing. But even something as seemingly reliable as vision may not be as dependable as you've thought.

To demonstrate, take a piece of blank paper and roll it up, hot dog style, as though it's a telescope. Hold your makeshift telescope up to your left eye in your left hand. Place your right hand against the side of the tube, fingers together and palm flat, about halfway between the eyehole and end of the "telescope." Now, close your right eye only and look through your telescope with your left eye. Your right hand should be in front of your closed eye. Now open your right eye.

What do you see?

Assuming that both of your eyes are working together—which is true for most people—it should appear as though there is a hole in your right hand. Don't worry, though, I didn't create a hole in your hand. If you open your left eye, the hole will disappear.

Okay—what just happened? If you have two eyes that work together, then your eyes are constantly receiving images of the world around you. For the most part, these images are *almost* identical. The main difference is that the object you are viewing exists at two slightly different angles from each of your eyes. The brain combines these two images and, in this process, you are better able to perceive depth. Stereoscopic vision. Groovy, right?

Unfortunately, when you feed the brain drastically different images, it gets confused. What it knows to do is to try to make sense of the two images. One eye sees a hole, and the other sees a hand. What emerges is the perception that you have a hole in your hand. Likewise, our brains can stretch or squash information gathered from the world around us until it is virtually unrecognizable.

Cognitive distortions are like lenses that get placed in front of our eyes without our knowledge. They morph the facts just like those fun house mirrors morph our reflections.

Each of these lenses has certain tells. When you view the world through rose-colored glasses, everything takes on a pink hue. If someone put these glasses on you while you were asleep, what would cue you to their presence when you awoke? Well, if you noticed that everything around you appeared pink, you'd probably assume that you were wearing rose-colored glasses. You'd use context clues.

Likewise, we want to practice identifying cognitive distortions using context cues. For example, let's say you text your friend, and they never get back to you. You might think, "They must be mad at me!" While your thoughts jumped to a conclusion, that if your friend didn't text you then they must be angry, this isn't the only explanation.

Our brains have a tendency to jump to conclusions. This makes sense in the context of our evolutionary past. You want to assume that the rustling in the bushes is something rather than nothing. After all, if you assume that the rustling is just the breeze rather than a hungry lion, you're less likely to survive in the instances when a predator is on the prowl. We are the ancestors of people who jumped to conclusions. In this episode of Survival of the Fittest, people who didn't jump to conclusions probably got "voted off the island."

If you understand that your brain is full of thoughts, then you will be aware that "they must be mad at me!" is a series of words that crossed your mind. If you understand your thoughts tend toward certain errors, like jumping to conclusions, you can take this into consideration when weighing whether these thoughts get to inform your behaviors.

Let's consider some of the common lenses that come up with OCD as well as their tells.

Common Cognitive Distortions in OCD

All-or-None Thinking

Seeing the world in extremes, as black and white, and ignoring the middle ground—the gray area. Also called dichotomous thinking.

The tell: If you're using words like "never," "always," "everyone," and "everything," you might be stuck in all-or-none thinking.

How is your thinking all-or-none?

___

___

Jumping to Conclusions

Deciding you know what something means without considering all the facts.

The tell: You may find yourself saying things like "This must mean…" Your statements will likely be definitive, without room for other conclusions or possibilities.

How do you jump to conclusions?

___

___

Fortune Telling

Predicting one outcome without recognizing that there are other possible outcomes.

The tell: You're spinning stories of what the future is destined to look like even though you haven't mastered the art of reading crystal balls.

This might sound like "I won't be able to handle it when…" or "I'm going to fail." The statement will likely be definitive even though it's not possible for you to know how things will turn out.

What fortunes does your mind tell?

___

___

Labeling

Putting a fixed label on a person and ignoring the fact that people are not so easily categorized.

The tell: Usually, there's a lot of name-calling going on. Think "I'm bad," "He's an idiot," or "Why can't I just be normal?"

What labels does your mind place on yourself or others?

___

___

Confirmation Bias

Giving greater credence to evidence in your environment that confirms your preexisting beliefs.

The tell: You'll notice that you discount evidence against your beliefs—using the words "Yeah, but..." You also respond with anecdotes that align with your beliefs, even those beliefs that you don't want to be true.

How does confirmation bias operate in your mind?

___

___

Mind Reading

Assuming you know what others are thinking or feeling.

The tell: You've decided what another person's perspective is even though you haven't discussed it with that person.

This probably sounds like "They obviously think..."

How do you mind read?

___

___

Personalizing

Believing that things are happening in a certain way because of you.

The tell: You presume that you've influenced something that happened with little to no evidence that whatever happened has anything to do with you. For example, you believe someone is upset with you because they haven't responded to a text.

How do you personalize things?

____

____

"Should" Statements

Having rigid expectations about how things "should" be.

The tell: You'll notice the word "should" a lot. You might also notice judgments like "It's not normal that..."

What "should" statements come up for you?

____

____

Comparison

Contrasting your experience with others' experiences in a way that devalues yours.

The tell: You may find yourself considering just how wonderful things would be if they were a certain way or explaining how it's not fair that others have one experience while you have another.

How does comparison show up for you?

____

____

Emotional Reasoning

Believing your feelings indicate how accurate your thoughts are.

The tell: You're using phrases like "It feels so real!" or "But I feel like…"

How do you engage in emotional reasoning?

____

____

Hyper-Responsibility

Having an inflated sense of responsibility with regard to causing or preventing negative outcomes.

The tell: Your thoughts may include phrases like "It's all my fault" or "I can't let that happen."

How does hyper-responsibility arise in your thoughts?

____

____

Recognizing Distortions

Let's return to the example above where you jumped to conclusions about why your friend hasn't responded to your text. If you let that thought inform your behavioral choices, you might find yourself in an internal debate about why your friend would be mad at you. You might concoct an entire argument against your friend, explaining why their anger isn't warranted and why it's *their* fault that they're mad at you. You could beat up on yourself for hours, recounting the ways in which you are a subpar friend. Ultimately, though, this is all an illusion. You've spent a ton of time trying to resolve a problem that may not actually exist.

If, instead, you recognize that you've jumped to a conclusion, you might see that your thought isn't necessarily the truth. Your friend could be mad at you, but other alternatives could be true. Your friend might be busy or may be trying to get an answer to your question. Once you're aware of other possibilities, you might be more willing to drop out of mental behaviors aimed at addressing the possibility that your friend is mad at you.

You can also take pause when you're having a strong emotional response and ask yourself, *What just went through my mind?* Oftentimes, you will find that you've been listening to an unpleasant story in your brain that makes use of some of these cognitive distortions. For instance, you might have predicted what's bound to happen in the future—fortune telling. If you've been unwittingly listening to an inner doom-and-gloom radio station, you can see where you might start to have a strong emotional response. Knowing how thoughts impact feelings, we can see strong emotions as signs to check in with our thinking. By checking in with our thinking, we get to make deliberate choices about whether our thoughts inform the choices we make.

What to Do with Distortions

So how do we stop distortions from ruling our lives and making our choices for us? In short, cognitive restructuring: a process by which we reconsider unhelpful thoughts.

Cognitive restructuring involves vetting thoughts much like you might vet that clickbait article on your social media feed. If everyone immediately bought into all the news stories showing up in their feeds, they might assume that Bigfoot was real and wholly avoid the Pacific Northwest (which would be a real shame since it's a beautiful area!) Likewise, we don't want you to miss out on the beautiful moments of your life just because your brain can concoct scary, unsubstantiated stories. We want you to consider if it makes sense to let these stories impact your behaviors.

The process begins by comparing your thinking pattern against the established thinking patterns detailed above—cognitive distortions. As we've discussed, by identifying the distortion, we are better able to consider whether our thoughts are likely to be warped or accurate representations of reality. This is akin to seeing a headline that's a bit outlandish and recognizing that you might want to consider the source.

Once we've identified that there is a distortion at play, a few considerations can help guide our behaviors.

Question 1: Is the thought likely to be true?

If we are having difficulty determining whether a thought is likely to reflect reality, we can consider how reasonable, rational, or logical it is *once*. Why once? We'll get to that shortly. In the meantime, keep in mind that our goal is **not** to prove whether a thought is true or false. Our goal is to gather information so we can make our best guess about how to move forward.

If you are unclear about the likelihood of a possibility that has occurred to you, consider the questions in the list that follows. While you review these questions, keep a few things in mind. First, feelings aren't evidence. When walking through this process, imagine that you are presenting the evidence to a jury. Would it stand up as evidence under scrutiny in a courtroom? Also, rationality and logic aren't subjective. They are objective. Therefore, if you say, "It's rational to me," there's a high likelihood that you're consulting your feelings rather than rationality.

Consider the following questions as you determine your best guess about the likelihood of the thought:

- Is this concern reasonable, rational, and logical? Would others consider it to be reasonable, rational, and logical? If someone else had this concern, would I judge it as reasonable, rational, and logical?

  ____

  ____

- What evidence do I have for or against this possibility? If I shared this with someone else, would they agree with my assessment? What assessment would I make if someone else had this evidence?

  ____

  ____

  ____

  ____

Accessing rationality, logic, and reason is key in recovery as we're better off letting likelihoods make our choices than we are letting remote possibilities make our decisions. That doesn't mean, however, that looking at rationality is without its issues.

Cognitive restructuring can be a tricky business for people with OCD. This process of restructuring can easily turn into an endless mental debate or mental reassurance, and thus you get stuck in mental compulsions.

Given that research has found that self-reassurance is one of the most common forms of mental compulsion (Pal et al. 2024), those who are prone to mental compulsions are wise to tread lightly when considering these cognitive skills. We could easily get lost in rationalizing why we needn't worry, which is still keeping us trapped in our own minds. So, if you're tempted to restructure the same thought multiple times, be wary. You may be using this practice compulsively.

That's why, when we're restructuring, we are wise to acknowledge the possibilities that come into our awareness however likely or unlikely they may be. To demonstrate using an earlier example, let's say you assume that your friend is mad at you when they don't respond to your text. When we acknowledge other possibilities in this case, we are not saying that your friend isn't mad at you. We don't know if your friend is mad at you. We are merely recognizing that if other possibilities appear to be likely, it doesn't make sense to act as though the first possibility or worst case is accurate.

If we don't have evidence that your friend is mad, then it's not rational to act as though they're mad. Given this, you want to *behave* as though your friend is not angry with you. This means no apologizing, reassurance seeking, or ruminating to determine how they might feel. We also want to acknowledge that the conclusion you jumped to *could* be right. That's because when we accept that all things are possible, we inoculate ourselves against the perpetual mental back-and-forth that keeps us out of the present moment.

At the risk of putting too fine a point on it, we restructure not to rationalize away emotions but, instead, to make choices that are aligned with the facts. This is down to changing how we behave, not how we feel. If you find yourself getting stuck in a back-and-forth, then skip this step and move on to question two.

Question 2: Would a response be helpful?

Let's say that you determine that an outcome is likely. For instance, you may have existential obsessions and be plagued with thoughts about your parents' mortality. When you consider whether an outcome is likely, you'll probably recognize that it is likely that your parents will die before you do. If this is likely, then doesn't a response make sense?

Not necessarily. This is where the question "Would a response be helpful?" becomes important. Would it be helpful for you to respond to the thought that your parents will die before you by ruminating about this? Well, no amount of rumination will "fix" your parents' mortality or the likelihood that they will die before you. Ruminating won't help you achieve a different outcome. Some might argue that thinking about their mortality in advance could reduce the pain associated with the loss. Even so, losing a loved one is difficult and any possible benefit of "preparing yourself" would be marginal at best.

So, do we think that rumination is helpful? The answer is a resounding "no."

Take a moment to go back and review your mental compulsions from chapter 1. Are these behaviors helpful?

____

____

____

Question 3: Would a response serve your values?

To determine whether a response to a thought serves your values, we must first establish what we mean by values. In this context, we are talking about values from an acceptance and commitment therapy (ACT) perspective. Within ACT, values are defined as the qualities that you most want to embody. The following exercise will help you get an idea of what values matter to you.

Determining your values. Take a moment to think of a person you deeply admire, aspire to be more like, or look up to. What is it about this person that inspires you? Maybe they regularly engage in acts of service—they are generous with their time. They might be warm—quick to smile and offer words of support. Perhaps you appreciate the presence they bring to conversations or the patience they demonstrate when speaking with children. Jot down some qualities you associate with them:

___

___

___

___

Consider now: Are these qualities that you want to stand for? Is this how you'd like people to remember you? Use the space provided to list the qualities that are meaningful and important to you.

___

___

___

___

___

Review the list you've created and ask yourself whether you have the ability to embody these qualities regardless of circumstances. For example, if you value being kind, are you always capable of being kind? Absolutely. It may be more or less difficult depending on circumstances, but the choice to center kindness is always within your control. If you've listed something like "financial success," this is not something that you can always attain, regardless of circumstances. Building financial success is a goal that you can work toward; persistence and diligence are values you can always prioritize whether you're financially successful or not.

List the remaining qualities that are, in fact, values:

___

___

___

___

___

Now for the hardest part: picking the most important values. Which ones are your nonnegotiable priorities?

One person's top five values might look like this:

- Light-hearted
- Open-minded
- Compassionate
- Creative
- Curious

And another person's might look like this:

- Silly
- Courageous
- Thorough
- Flexible
- Gentle

One person might find all of these qualities to be admirable. I know I do. But different people rank different qualities as more important to them. What five of the ones you've written are *most* important to you?

____

____

Much of the time, your values won't be in conflict, so you won't have to stick to this shortened list. But there will be times where you are faced with prioritizing one value over the other. Perhaps you're up against a deadline at work. Are you willing to be unkind toward yourself in pursuit of being thorough? Or are you willing to be less thorough if it means prioritizing kindness? In these moments, knowing which values are most important to you will be key.

Paring down the list of values can be helpful even as a temporary exercise. Tracking *all* of the qualities you value can be overwhelming and shortening this list can help maintain focus with prioritizing these qualities.

The beauty of values is that we always have the power to express them. So many things in life are beyond our control because so many variables can impact outcomes. How we show up to any situation is one of the few things we can control. And if we consistently prioritize our values, we will be content with our choices even if the outcomes aren't as we hoped.

If your behaviors aren't aligned with your values, you won't be content with your own actions when you achieve your goals. You may be happy about the destination you reached, but you won't be happy with the road you took.

What does all of this have to do with cognitive restructuring? Well, if an action does not serve our values, then we are better off making a different choice. Let's return to our example of the person with existential OCD who ruminates about their parents' deaths. If they asked themselves, *Does this action serve my values?*, how might they respond? First, they'd need to consider what qualities matter most to them. Most people value being present given that life only ever happens in the here and now. If we presume they value being present, then they probably don't want to waste time ruminating about a future they can't resolve. This would be an "away move," as it would take the person further from their values. Indeed, such mental compulsions would only take them further into the recesses of their minds, away from the present where their parents are alive. Does a behavioral response serve their values and the person that they want to be? No. However, reorienting toward the present and their experience with their parents would be considered a "toward move," helping them to get closer toward the person they want to be.

In ACT, the concept of toward and away moves is often depicted as a bullseye with the value in the middle. A toward move would take you closer to the value and the away move moves you further away from the value.

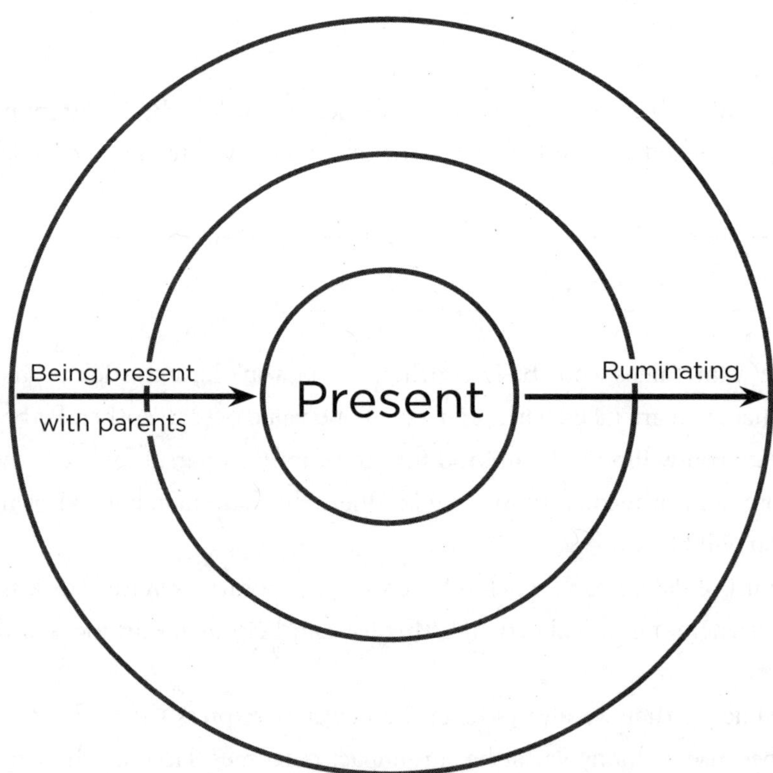

Now consider whether those mental compulsions you wrote down in chapter 1 serve your values. Do they get you closer to the person you want to be? Or do they take you further away from what matters to you? Perhaps it takes you closer to some while taking you further from others. Jot your thoughts down.

____

____

____

____

____

____

After Restructuring

Once you have answered these questions, you can make a more thoughtful choice about how to respond to thoughts. In short, if you answer "no" to any of the questions, then a behavioral response is unlikely to be in your best interest.

I use the term "unlikely" here particularly for those whose OCD centers on doubt. Restructuring is intended to help us find clarity about which path will *likely* benefit us overall rather than to provide certainty. We may still feel doubt about our decision because it's still possible that a behavioral response could be beneficial. Restructuring is a bridge that makes the leap of accepting uncertainty a little narrower and less daunting. Even so, there will still be a leap involved as you accept your emotional experiences in the service of acting in a way that makes sense.

The next chapters will explore how we can use mindfulness to support our acceptance of thoughts, feelings, urges, and sensations, and thus support us in taking the leap.

Questioning Distortions

Now, putting all the questions together, you can use the following worksheet to question distortions when they arise. You can also print a copy of this worksheet at http://www.newharbinger.com/55541.

The thought: ____

____

____

Question 1: Is the thought likely to be true?

- Is this concern reasonable, rational, and logical? Would others consider it to be reasonable, rational, and logical? If someone else had this concern, would I judge it as reasonable, rational, and logical?

  ___

  ___

- What evidence do I have for or against this possibility? If I shared this with someone else, would they agree with my assessment? What assessment would I make if someone else had this evidence?

  ___

  ___

  ___

  ___

Question 2: Would a response be helpful?

Are these behaviors helpful?

___

___

___

Question 3: Would a response serve your values?

Does a response get you closer to the person you want to be? Or take you further away from what matters to you?

___

___

___

___

After Restructuring

Once you have answered these questions, you can make a more thoughtful choice about how to respond to thoughts. In short, if you answer "no" to any of the questions, then a behavioral response is unlikely to be in your best interest.

Chapter 6

The What and Why of Mindfulness

There are a lot of misunderstandings about mindfulness. Given its association with eastern philosophy and Buddhism, many people think mindfulness requires a Zen-like calm. The concept may bring to mind an image of a monk sitting in the lotus position with his eyes closed, breathing deeply, feeling completely mellow, and maybe even levitating. I am sorry to disappoint, but despite years of meditation practice, I have yet to levitate. While few people likely expect they will actually lift off the ground while meditating, they might genuinely think these other stereotypes associated with "mindfulness" are necessary parts of the practice. This can lead people to stop soon after they've begun because they think they're "bad at mindfulness."

So, let's begin by addressing these misunderstandings. First, mindfulness doesn't guarantee feelings of bliss or happiness. Jon Kabat-Zinn defines mindfulness as the awareness that arises when one pays attention to the present moment in a nonjudgmental fashion (Kabat-Zinn 1994). And being aware of the present moment nonjudgmentally often involves recognizing experiences that we might categorize as "bad." When sadness arises, mindfulness acknowledges its existence without passing judgment. This might sound like "Oh, I'm feeling sadness" rather than "Ugh, I'm feeling sad again. I hate sadness! I wish it would go away."

Likewise, when thoughts arise that we wouldn't choose, the practice of mindfulness involves awareness of those thoughts. You can practice mindfulness by adding the phrase "I'm having the thought that..." to the beginning of whatever thought you have. This approach also applies to urges and images. The hope is to develop a more peaceful relationship with our internal experiences by withholding judgment rather than forcing ourselves to feel joy.

Also, mindfulness isn't about breathing! People often confuse mindfulness with breathing exercises. This is likely because mindfulness meditation instructions often involve grounding your attention, mindfully, in your experience of breathing. Even here, though, the breath is only a proxy for your present moment experience. It's not about the breath but rather about delving into your sensory experience of the here and now.

Also, you don't have to practice formal, seated meditation to practice mindfulness. Meditation can be an incredible way to support mindfulness and help those struggling with mental compulsions. Unfortunately, a lot of people have misgivings about meditation. As a result, meditation might turn people off from the practice of mindfulness, leading them to miss out on its benefits altogether.

You may still think mindfulness and meditation are remote practices—fodder for monks or dedicated practitioners. But one need not be of any religious leaning or expertise to embrace their value. In fact, when we apply mindfulness to thoughts, emotions, sensations, and urges, it's exceedingly practical. What's more, mindfulness-based therapies are effective in supporting people with OCD (Chien et al. 2022; Ricquelme-Marín 2022).

Mindfulness, OCD, and Response Prevention

In OCD recovery, we practice mindfulness to foster acceptance of thoughts, emotions, sensations, and urges that we tend to resist. When we're unwilling to have thoughts, feelings, urges, and sensations, we resist them. Our resistance to these experiences leads us to do things to get rid of them—things we wouldn't otherwise do. These behavioral responses interfere with us living our lives. If I'm unwilling to have thoughts about being a serial killer and related feelings of fear, then I might spend hours in my head ruminating about whether I could be a serial killer. These hours spent ruminating distract me from being present in my life.

While resistance leads to compulsions, mindfulness, especially the element of nonjudgment, supports acceptance. This acceptance equates to reduced resistance and, therefore, reduced compulsions. Thus, mindfulness supports response prevention.

How Does Resistance Increase Your Compulsions?

Take a moment to reflect on the following statements and fill in the blanks based on your experience. This will help you better appreciate the connection between being unwilling to have an experience, resisting that experience, and compulsions.

I have been unwilling to have thoughts, including ______________________________

____

I have been unwilling to have feelings, including ______________________________

____

I have been unwilling to have urges and sensations like __________________________

____

As a result, I ______________________________

mental compulsions I perform

These mental compulsions interfere with my life by ______________________________

____

As you can see, practicing nonjudgmental awareness, or mindfulness, of experiences supports acceptance of them. If I notice my thoughts about being a serial killer and my corresponding feelings of anxiety with an attitude of curiosity, I can choose to let them exist. Once we accept thoughts, feelings, urges, and sensations, *we* get to choose which actions we take. We are free to live life on our own terms rather than at the ever-changing whim of our internal experiences.

A Glimpse into Acceptance

Take a moment to reflect on the following statements and fill in the blanks according to your experience. This will help you better appreciate the connection between being willing to have an experience, accepting that experience, and the ability to prioritize the behaviors that matter to you.

I am having the thought that ______________________________

____

I am noticing I'm feeling ______________________________

I am noticing ______________________________

sensations and urges

I am willing to have these experiences so that I can ______________________________

____

The Building Blocks of Mindfulness

Now that we understand how mindfulness might be useful, let's consider why the three components of mindfulness—awareness, present moment, and nonjudgment—are important in the practice.

Awareness

When I ask people what mindfulness means, "awareness" is one of the first answers I get. This makes sense. When "mindfulness" is used conversationally, it's often used as a synonym for awareness. If someone tells you to be mindful of someone's emotions, they are likely suggesting that you be aware and thoughtful of their feelings.

While awareness is not the only facet of mindfulness, it is a big part of the picture. As we've discussed, when we are not aware that our thoughts are thoughts, we tend to accept them at face value and be enormously impacted by them. Essentially, when we are unaware of our thoughts, then they function as our reality. If you have the thought *You're likely to murder someone if you drive a car,* and you never stop to acknowledge that this is a thought, then this thought is more likely to be treated as fact and to keep you from driving.

When you become the witness of your thoughts, then they don't necessarily get to make your choices for you. Your awareness allows you to make decisions based on what matters to you.

As we've covered, being unaware of emotions, sensations, and urges can be just as problematic. A lack of awareness might lead us to think of feelings or urges as facts too. If you feel anxious, for example, but you are unaware of the fact that you are experiencing an emotion, you are likely to interpret the experience of urgency that accompanies anxiety as a signal of danger. Even if there are no genuine indicators of danger in your environment, your emotions, unexamined, can lead you to act as though you are in danger. Yes, without awareness, we are at the whim of our internal experiences, which is part of the reason why we want to dig into mindfulness practice.

Present Moment

The present moment is where the meat of life is. I'm fond of a Sanskrit proverb that reads: "For yesterday is but a dream, and tomorrow is only a vision." The experience of life, however, is now. As the quote continues: "Today, well lived, makes every yesterday a dream of happiness and every tomorrow a vision of hope."

As I write these words on this page, I can hear the clacking of the smooth keys underneath my fingers. I can hear the hum of a fan in the background. I can feel an itch on my middle finger. I see the letters appearing on the screen and taste coffee on my breath. Out of the corner of my eye, I notice the movement of green leaves outside of my window. This is my present moment experience. Right now, the rest of my life is either a dream or a vision. My husband, children, friends, and family are only memories. What could happen tomorrow is merely an unwritten story and what happened last year is an increasingly vague recollection.

Being able to connect to my present moment experience is the essence of life. Of course, I plan for the future and reflect on the past from time to time. But these reflections and musings can easily devolve, overtaking every moment in which I might otherwise live. Consider that experiencing what *is*, whether we categorize it as "good" or "bad," is how we savor the fleeting, ephemeral experience of being alive.

Besides, thinking excessively about the future or past often gives way to intense emotions like anxiety and sadness. While trying to get rid of feelings isn't wise, doing something that doesn't serve us and exacerbates challenging emotions isn't wise either. If you're looking to minimize emotions like anxiety, practicing orienting toward the present moment is your jam! Being aware of your emotion in the present, nonjudgmentally, has the strange effect of helping those emotions settle more easily.

Getting Present

You may now be wondering how in the world you can simply "be present." One helpful way to get into your experience of the here and now is to ground in your five senses. Next time you're worrying about what will happen next year or what went on in the meeting you had last week, you can use the following sensory grounding exercise. This will help get you back in contact with the present moment. All you need to remember is 3, 2, 1.

3: Nonjudgmentally, name 3 things in your environment that you can see, feel, and hear

2: Nonjudgmentally, name 2 different things in your environment that you can see, feel, and hear

1: Nonjudgmentally, name 1 different thing in your environment that you can see, feel, and hear

Chances are, after that exercise, you're more engaged with your immediate experiences. All that nonjudgmental noticing helped you get in contact with the present moment.

Nonjudgment

Our tendency is to place judgment on our thoughts and feelings. Of course, as we've discussed, snap judgments of catastrophe have helped people survive and pass on their genes. If our ancestors had lingered around assuming that the rustling in the bushes was a deer, they would have increased their likelihood of becoming bear lunch. Hence, we judge.

Sound = Bear = Bad = Bolt

Nonjudgment vs. Judgment

To help you get a better sense of your judgments, let's help you practice noticing them. Consider the following prompts and answer the related questions. They are specifically designed to create judgments.

As you answer the questions and prompts, try to notice the judgments that arise in a nonjudgmental way. You can use phrases like:

- "Oh, I'm noticing that I'm judging this experience as [negative or positive]."
- "I'm noticing that I'm disliking [this]."
- "I'm noticing that I'm enjoying [this]."

Question: *What is one of your favorite foods?* ______________________________

Imagine for a moment that you are being served that food.

What does it smell like? ______________________________

What does it look like? ______________________________

Now imagine taking a bite.

What do you taste? ______________________________

What is the texture like? ______________________________

Question: *What is one of your* least *favorite foods?* ______________________________

Imagine for a moment that you are being served that food.

What does it smell like? ______________________________

What does it look like? ______________________________

Now imagine taking a bite.

What do you taste? ______________________________

What is the texture like? ______________________________

I invite you now to look back over your answers. Notice if there are words like "good," "bad," "delicious," or "disgusting." These words are judgments of the experience and are one step removed from the experience itself.

What do I mean by one step removed? Consider that if you only described the scent, taste, or visual aspect of a food using these judgments, it would be very difficult to guess what you were talking about. If I filled out those questions in a judgmental way using my least favorite food, it might look like this:

What does it smell like? *Awful*

What does it look like? *Disgusting*

What do you taste? *Nastiness*

What is the texture like? *Gross!*

You likely have no idea what kind of food I'm talking about. Indeed, our judgments tell us very little about the objective experience. What happens if I describe the experience more objectively?

What does it smell like? *It has a slightly sweet smell, though it's mostly briny.*

What does it look like? *The outside has a silvery sheen. The inside has a saturated pinkish hue.*

What do you taste? *The flavor, like the scent, is very briny.*

What is the texture like? *The texture is soft, flakey, and tender. It's also moist.*

This is likely to give you a better sense of what I'm talking about. You may not guess that my least favorite food is salmon, but you'd have a much better sense of my direct sensory experience.

If you noticed that you were very judgmental in your description, return to it now and consider what the experience is like when you omit the judgmental words. Do you find yourself wincing and writhing less in this process? That's because nonjudgment helps to reduce resistance.

Judgment → Resistance and Resistance → Suffering

When we judge something as bad, we resist it. Unfortunately, when it comes to things we can't manage and control directly—like thoughts and feelings—our resistance and clinging lead us to struggle. Hence the nonjudgmental part of mindfulness helps to reduce this unnecessary suffering we might add to whatever pain we experience—whether that suffering is as a direct result of compulsions or simply due to the discomfort of tension.

The ACT Pushing Away Paper Exercise

This exercise is adapted from Russ Harris (Harris 2021).

Grab a blank piece of paper.

Before you do anything with that piece of paper, look around you. Imagine, for a moment, that everything that matters to you is in front of you, beyond the piece of paper: the things that bring you joy—your favorite people, activities, places, foods, entertainment, and art—and the more difficult aspects of your life—the challenging undertakings and problems that need your direct attention.

Now imagine that all of your unwanted inner experiences are on this piece of paper: your uncomfortable thoughts, feelings, obsessions, and anxieties.

We've been taught that the best way to deal with these things is to try to rid ourselves of them, to get them as far away from us as possible. Let's try that now. Of course, since we can't get rid of these thoughts and feelings, we aren't allowed to put the paper down and run in the opposite direction. We can, however, try to push that paper away. So, hold it out—really get it as far away as you can!

This process of trying to avoid the internal experiences that we don't like can be challenging in and of itself. It can be:

- Exhausting: You may have noticed your muscles tense as you pushed that piece of paper away from you.
- Distracting: The piece of paper becomes the most predominant thing you can see and blocks out the rest of the world—including the things that matter most to you.
- Consuming: It's hard to go about your day or get things done when your priority is keeping that piece of paper as far away from you as possible.

But what if you let that piece of paper rest in your lap? What if you held that piece of paper as you go about your day? By allowing your internal experiences to be present, you have more energy and attention to engage with your life. You're no longer distracted by trying to rid yourself of discomfort, and you can funnel the energy you used avoiding inner experiences into engaging with your life.

Resisting things that you cannot change doesn't make sense because resistance doesn't get rid of internal experiences, AND it makes us subjectively feel worse. Moreover, as we briefly discussed at the start of this chapter, resistance increases behaviors like compulsions that interfere with our ability to live life on our terms. Let's continue exploring the liabilities of resistance so we can strengthen your resolve to practice nonjudgment and accept some uncomfortable experiences.

Thought Suppression and the Rebound Effect

Don't think about a green zebra.

What just happened?

Chances are you just thought of a green zebra. That's the rebound effect, brought to you by your attempt at thought suppression, courtesy of the first sentence. The whole basis of the concept is that in order to not think about something, you have to think about it. As such, trying not to think about something tends to make that thought more prevalent.

Resistance of Feelings

As with automatic thoughts, we can't control which emotions show up. Feelings are like the weather: ever-changing and inevitable. Would you resist the fact that it's raining? Most people can recognize how pointless this is. Sure, you might momentarily wish that the weather was sunny, but your ability to be present and live your best rainy day life is halted if you choose to continue wishing. You may still prefer sunny days to rainy ones just as you probably prefer joy to anxiety. But given that you can't control feelings, resisting them doesn't make sense.

When left to their own devices, emotions manage themselves. It's when we get involved in the natural process of feeling—for example, by performing mental compulsions—that we prolong and exacerbate emotions. Therefore, resisting emotions is both ineffective and unnecessary. You can remove that item from your to-do list. You've got enough on your plate!

Besides, you don't need to feel a certain way to behave a certain way. You can feel sad and still choose to get out of bed. You can feel angry and still practice patience. And you can feel afraid and keep doing the things that matter to you. Ultimately, resisting emotions only stands in the way of building a meaningful life.

Resistance Feels Similar to Distress

Resistance itself tends to be perceived as unpleasant. Think back to the last time you resisted an emotion. Was the resistance itself pleasant? The felt experience of resisting emotions generally involves tightening, tension, constriction, and discomfort. You can probably attest to this if you did the pushing away paper exercise on the preceding pages. (If you didn't actually do the exercise, I encourage you to go back and do it now.) This tightness, tension, and constriction is what makes the resistance *more* uncomfortable. Indeed, the felt experience of resistance shares a lot of similarities with emotions like anxiety or distress. Tension, for example, occurs in both. Thus, in trying not to feel distress, you may perceive that you are experiencing more distress.

The Second Arrow

Mindfulness helps us keep the pain inherent to life from getting worse. One need not make the emotions they're feeling more pronounced by resisting them or make thoughts more persistent by trying to make them go away. Resistance is, ultimately, a demonstration of shooting the second arrow.

Arrows? Where did arrows come from? I'll explain: There is a parable of two arrows. The first arrow represents the pain we cannot control. The second arrow represents the suffering caused by our reaction to the inevitable pain of life. The core question of the parable? "If you get hit with an arrow, do you then shoot a second arrow into yourself?"

If you're disappointed because you'd like to do something but are unable to—that's the first arrow. But if you then begin to judge your disappointment, wondering what's wrong with you that you can't just be grateful for what you have, that's the second arrow. Given that the second arrow increases pain and won't decrease the pain of automatic thoughts, feelings, urges, and sensations, it makes more sense to accept these experiences.

Resistance Interferes with Life

We can prioritize attempts to diminish and rid ourselves of feelings, or we can prioritize the actions that are meaningful to us. When these two things come into conflict, which they often do, then the priority will determine how we act.

So, if I have distress and prioritize resisting distress, then I will perform compulsions that often run counter to how I want to live my life. If I'm anxious that I don't know my "true" sexual orientation, then I may spend hours trying to get rid of my anxiety by analyzing what my feelings mean about my sexuality. In the meantime, I'll be missing out on the present moment.

Just as the piece of paper stands in the way of what matters in life, attempts to get rid of distress interfere with our ability to create a fulfilling life.

Attitudes Toward Emotions that Support Nonjudgment

We've established that resistance isn't the answer and that nonjudgment and acceptance can support OCD recovery. Still, the way our culture talks about emotions is highly judgmental and reflects a larger societal tendency to resist certain feelings. In light of this, let's address some cultural misconceptions about emotions to support you in approaching your emotions nonjudgmentally.

All Feelings Are Valid

Conventional "wisdom" suggests that if feelings don't make sense, then they aren't valid. If you've ever been told to stop feeling sad or that you shouldn't feel anxious, you can appreciate how ridiculous this is. If we could stop emotions by rationalizing with them, then no one would be reading this book. The belief that emotions should be rational is, actually, irrational.

This attitude leads right into resistance. If you believe that you shouldn't feel whatever emotion you're feeling, then you're going to try to fix your feelings, and, as we've established, that doesn't work. Emotions and rationality both have their place, and the legitimacy of either doesn't hinge on our ability to reconcile the two.

All feelings are valid, and all feelings deserve our compassion even if we can't make logical sense of them.

Feelings Don't Have to Make Sense

Consider a baby or a small child. One moment they're happy as a clam, and the next they're wailing. You may change them, feed them, and try to rock them to sleep to no avail. You may even talk to them about their feelings and what's leading them to have certain emotional experiences. Can you think of a time in your life when you've seen a baby or young child having a big emotional response?

____

____

Now consider if their emotional response seemed appropriate to the situation. For instance, if you saw a child at the grocery store sobbing as they pleaded to their parent for a toy at the checkout, was this a reasonable response or did it seem excessive to you?

____

____

Now consider whether you believe that the feeling was authentic. Did the baby or child in your experience seem to be genuinely upset?

____

____

While the intensity of their sadness may not have made logical sense, they were undoubtedly feeling whatever they were feeling. And trying to talk them out of whatever they were feeling likely wouldn't take away the emotional experience.

Given this, consider if you were caring for that child. Would you tell them not to feel sad? Would you yell at them about how their feeling doesn't make sense? Or might you acknowledge their feelings and help them to accept these feelings while asserting your behavioral expectations? The latter might sound like "I hear that you're really upset, and also we're not getting that toy. It's difficult to feel frustrated. I'm here for you as you feel that frustration. Remember though, we don't yell at each other just because we're frustrated." Consider what you think a helpful response might sound like.

____

____

____

____

You can offer these same words to yourself in the face of emotions. You can give yourself the same compassion that you might offer to that child even if you can't make sense of how you're feeling. You can also hold yourself to a standard while accepting the emotion. Thus, you can be kind and firmly commit to your choice to drop compulsions.

Feelings Aren't Good or Bad

If I asked you to categorize feelings as good or bad, you'd probably be able to in no time flat! Think of all the rhetoric you've heard over a lifetime that's cultivated this ability:

"You're crying?! Don't be weak!"

"Scaredy cat! You're such a baby!"

"Don't doubt yourself. People won't like you if you're insecure."

This is just a small sampling of countless messages we are subjected to over our lifetimes. But to say a feeling is bad is to suggest that it doesn't serve a purpose. To judge emotions so rashly completely ignores the function of emotions and the fact that they all have their place.

Feelings are signs. Some signs—like stop signs—give us important information. Other signs—like advertisements—not necessarily. As with signs more generally, we must consider whether our emotional signals warrant our ongoing attention or action. Emotions get our attention, and can give us valuable information, but emotions shouldn't get to make *all* of your decisions. The smoke detector going off doesn't necessarily mean fire. If you check for other signs of fire and don't find any, then it doesn't make sense to call the fire department. Not only would calling the fire department be unnecessary, it would cause a lot of hubbub and interfere with the firefighters' ability to fight an actual fire elsewhere. Likewise, if you respond to an emotion, like fear or disgust, without interpreting the sign, then you may take unnecessary and harmful actions. You might, for instance, ruminate excessively and intensify the emotions you're trying to avoid. This is why we want to learn how to consider rationality (see cognitive restructuring in chapter 5).

But this doesn't mean we should completely ignore emotions. While the signs aren't always right, they are still important. When used as an alert system rather than as proof of a problem, emotions can offer valuable information. Take, for example, the case of someone with Urbach-Wiethe disease, a rare condition that sometimes results in calcification of the amygdala. One individual with this disease doesn't have a functioning amygdala in either side of her brain and does not experience fear in many situations that typically cause fear. Her alarm system doesn't work, which has likely made her more vulnerable to the trauma she has experienced.

Have No Fear

Imagine for a moment that you didn't have any fear. As you went throughout your daily life, what would change? If you were tired and didn't want to wake up, would you simply stay in bed and miss work? If you remembered you needed something while in the shower, would you walk quickly across tiles with wet feet and slip? Would you grab the coffee pot by its base and burn your hand? Would you text while driving during your morning commute? Jot down your thoughts.

____

____

____

____

____

____

Sure, you might have a rational understanding about the likely consequences of your actions, but chances are that if you never felt fear, you would be more impulsive and find yourself in more dangerous situations.

While it may be tempting to paint some emotions as "bad," all emotions are important. It's not just with fear or distress. Anger may indicate that our boundaries are being violated. Sadness may indicate that we would benefit from social support. We just have to remember that the key word here is "may."

Can you think of a time when your anxiety aligned with the facts of a circumstance? Perhaps you chose not to walk alone down a dark alley at night or slowed down your car when you realized you'd passed the speed limit. Are you glad that your anxiety alerted you to the potential for danger?

When we can appreciate the reasons behind the experiences our minds generate, we can better accept the parts that we might otherwise judge. We'll more readily accept emotions, which will help us to disengage from unhelpful behaviors aimed at getting rid of feelings (I'm looking at you, mental compulsions).

I want to reiterate here that rationally reading the signs that precede emotions doesn't mean that our feelings will change. It simply means that we will have the chance to determine how to act effectively in the face of our feelings so that our lives aren't limited.

Yes, all emotions have their place. It's just that, when they come up, we want to keep them in their place. "Keeping them in their place" involves thoughtfully considering how they impact our actions, if at all. That's because while feelings *can* be important signs, they don't always provide us with actionable information.

The function of emotions is good even if we might view them as negative. More than that, though, if we look at emotions for what they really are—the combination of different physical sensations in the body—we can see that the physical sensations themselves are neither good nor bad. For instance, the physical sensations associated with anxiety, excitement, and falling in love are largely the same. The butterflies you might experience while falling in love are perceived as pleasant, while butterflies when feeling anxiety are considered unpleasant. Either way, though, they are the same physical sensation and, therefore, aren't inherently pleasant or unpleasant. Why would we, then, waste our time judging them?

Acceptance is the Answer

Bottom line: Anxiety and distress aren't all bad, and going to battle with emotions is akin to yelling at a guard dog for barking at someone who's walking down the street. Both the guard dog's bark and your distress serve a purpose.

What's more, resistance, whether of thoughts, feelings, urges, or sensations, causes so many issues while also being completely ineffective and unnecessary. Nonjudgment and acceptance are the way forward. So, what does nonjudgment of our present moment experiences look like? The next chapter will consider the practical application of mindfulness in the context of obsessions, emotions, and mental compulsions.

Chapter 7

Mindfulness Skills for Acceptance

There is a quote that perfectly summarizes what mindfulness affords its practitioners. It reads: "Between stimulus and response, there is a space. In that space is our power to choose our response. In our response lies our growth and our freedom" (Covey, et al. 1996, p. 59). Mindfulness allows us to access that space between being triggered and falling into mental compulsions. By noticing our internal experiences without judgment, by acknowledging and accepting what *is*, we create a moment in which we can make a different choice and overcome deeply ingrained behavioral patterns. Thus, nonjudgment leads to acceptance, which allows for response prevention, and, ultimately, freedom from the tyranny of mental compulsions.

Now that we've established why mindfulness is a useful practice for people with OCD, let's talk about *how* you can practice mindfulness to better navigate mental compulsions. This How section will be split up into two main subsections: chapter 7 will focus on mindfulness skills that support acceptance and chapter 8 will cover mindfulness tools that aid in both acceptance and refocusing attention. Both chapters will support you in practicing response prevention with mental compulsions.

Cognitive Defusion

Cognitive defusion, a core practice within ACT, involves taking a step back from your thoughts and observing them with objectivity. Instead of being "fused" with your thoughts, we want to help you "de-fuse" from them. Defusion is also sometimes referred to as deliteralization. I like this term because it gets to the heart of this practice. We want to stop taking our thoughts literally, as though the ideas they represent are necessarily factual. As we've discussed, thoughts may be representations of fact or fiction, but, one way or another, they are only representations.

Here are some defusion exercises for you to try out with your obsessions. Again, the aim here is to help you get some space from these words in your mind so that you can make deliberate choices as to how, and if, you respond. Thus, defusion can support response prevention.

Noticing

Start by repeatedly thinking about your obsession for ten seconds straight, focusing all of your attention on it. For instance, if you have harm OCD, this could sound like *I might harm my family, I might harm my family...*

After trying this, consider what you notice about your experience of this thought.

Now try repeating the phrase "I'm having the thought that [insert obsession here]" for ten seconds. For example, "I'm having the thought that I might harm my family."

Consider what your experience is like after repeating this second phrase.

You probably experienced a greater sense of distance from the thoughts after repeating the second phrase. Objectively observing your thoughts creates a moment of pause in which you can view these thoughts rather than engage with their content.

Mental Appreciation

Acknowledging your mind and its creativity is another defusion practice known as mental appreciation. This might sound like stating, nonsarcastically, *Brain! You're so creative. I don't know how you come up with this stuff. I'm always so impressed with how intensely realistic your imagination is.*

Why nonsarcastically? Well, the idea isn't to invalidate your thoughts, but to witness the process of having the thought. If you respond sarcastically, you're likely trying to talk yourself out of feelings by invalidating your thoughts. Translation: you're resisting the experience, thus keeping yourself stuck performing compulsions.

By acknowledging your brain's strengths, you're getting that mindful distance from your thoughts that will allow you to respond more thoughtfully and deliberately to them. You're also promoting a more congenial relationship with yourself and, ultimately, a friendlier environment in which you can live.

Consider what you might say to your brain the next time it comes up with a very creative obsession. Write it down in the space provided.

____

____

____

____

____

____

Sing It Out

You can sing your thoughts to the tune of a song. For instance, you could yodel the phrase "I might want to murder my dog!" to the melody of "Wrecking Ball." You could belt out the words "I could be totally immoral" to the tune of "Don't You Want Somebody to Love?"

Next time you're alone, take a minute to try this.

First, think of a song. Perhaps it's a dramatic ballad à la the band Chicago. Maybe it's an old-school Britney Spears pop hit. Once you've got that song, think of an intrusive thought you have regularly. Once you've got the thought, it's time to make your musical debut. Sing your thought to the tune of that song. You can do this in your head or out loud, whichever is your preference. Bonus points if you're not a particularly talented singer.

Again, the aim isn't to delegitimize your thoughts. While thoughts aren't inherently factual, defusion doesn't aim to disprove our thoughts. Instead, the aim is to recognize that thoughts are thoughts so we can respond to them in a way that serves us better.

Silly Voices

Are you any good at impressions? Boy, do I have the defusion exercise for you! Try on your best Mickey Mouse or Daffy Duck voice and have them narrate your intrusive thoughts. Maybe you've got a Christopher Walken that kills or a Matthew McConaughey that's dead on. (I find McConaughey pairs particularly well with existential obsessions.) You could invite Darth Vader to vocalize your thoughts on your behalf. Use your creative mind to help you step back and consider your thoughts for what they are: words in your mind.

Monsters on the Bus

Imagine you are a bus driver. You can drive any bus you like—a hippie bus covered in flowers, a tour bus adventuring through national parks, or a traditional school bus.

In this metaphor, the "bus" you're "driving" is actually a representation of you going about your life. You're in charge of charting your course, and you get to decide what direction you head in. Of course, having read this book, you know that you'll be most content if you choose to travel in the direction of your values. So, you start heading that way.

Maybe you're focused on being a loving person. You turn on the ignition and gear up to explore the embodiment of love—no matter if that love is directed toward yourself or someone else. The engine's humming, and you're puttering down the street toward love. You're smiling at the individuals passing by on the street, doing your utmost to exude warmth. At this point, you see a bus stop along the side of the road. You, the dutiful bus driver, come to a stop, open the doors, and idle for a moment.

Lo and behold, a would-be passenger steps right up. Ah, but this is no ordinary passenger. This is a monster. As it turns out, this monster is an obsession, so you start to hear the familiar drone in your ear of "what ifs" or start to see some uncomfortable images. Amid the cacophony of "what ifs," another monster rushes onto the bus. Oh look, it's anxiety! And she's got her longtime friends, heart palpitations and knots in the stomach tagging along. Self-criticism isn't far behind: *What's wrong with you? Why are you still having these thoughts?* It's getting crowded, and it's not the party bus that you might have planned for if you'd been sending out the invites. These monsters are persistent, and they're downright mean.

What's a bus driver to do? You could stay parked at this bus stop, trying to get these monsters off the bus. Unfortunately that would interfere with your ability to travel toward your values. Besides, these monsters aren't planning to exit anytime soon. Fighting them won't get them off the bus; it'll just make you more frustrated.

You could start yelling at these thoughts, feelings, and sensations as you drive, trying to get them to quiet down. But meeting these passengers—or your own internal world—in that way isn't all that loving. In navigating the bus ride this way, you would, essentially, be veering off course, away from your values.

You're also more likely to miss out on opportunities to center your values if you're busy planning on how to shut these guys up. So long as you're focused on them, you'll have less focus available to develop the kind of person you want to be.

Your best bet is to call out "All aboard!" in your most convincing conductor voice (because, why not?) and get this show on the road. You can acknowledge the monsters are there without getting into fights with them and continue driving toward your values once more. You might even express love toward yourself as the first step: *Wow—you're going through a lot. It's tough being on the bus with these guys. I'm really proud of you for showing up and being the person that you want to be even with all of these monsters yelling at you.* You might notice pride and compassion step on board at the next stop.

Along the journey, other monsters may hop on. Wave hello to the thoughts about how much better the bus ride would be without anxiety. Welcome the feelings of sadness about the obsessions that have come onboard. But whatever you do, keep your focus on living the kind of life you want to live and being the kind of person you want to be. That's how you get more of the passengers you like on the bus, anyway.

Nonengagement Responses

As with cognitive defusion, nonengagement responses support us in mindfully witnessing and accepting thoughts, feelings, and other internal experiences, thus paving the way for response prevention. You might wonder how you can respond without engaging. It sounds like an oxymoron. A nonengagement response is a response that addresses the *process* of OCD rather than the *content* of an obsession. Think back to our discussion of process and content in chapter 2. The content of the thoughts is what the thoughts are about. The process refers to experiencing obsessions, feeling discomfort, and attempting to resolve the distress obsessions generate. So, a nonengagement response acknowledges thoughts while sidestepping any longer dialogue with the thought.

If someone is struggling with real event OCD, they would first mindfully acknowledge that thoughts and fear have arisen: *Oh, I'm feeling fear because I've had this thought that I don't know whether that really happened.* From there, this person would make the choice to go ahead with their day. To support this, they might use a nonengagement response like *I'm not going to figure that out.* We're addressing the urge to figure it out, the feeling, the thought, and the uncertainty without actually interacting with the content of the thought.

"I'm not going to figure that out" is one of my favorite nonengagement responses. Given the role uncertainty plays in OCD, it often comes in handy when making the choice to disengage from mental compulsions. Whenever you want to answer the question embedded in an obsession, you can make a conscious decision to leave the question unanswered.

Sometimes, responding to our mind's anxious queries with "I'm not going to figure that out *right now*" can seem more accessible. This small change in verbiage nods to the reality that recovery only happens one decision at a time. We don't have to commit to not figuring it out forever, just right now. And right now. And right now.

"I don't know" is another great nonengagement response. It acknowledges the uncertainty and the commitment to leave that uncertainty unresolved.

Some other nonengagement responses include:

It's a mystery.

Who knows?

I guess we'll see.

Good to see you, guilt.

I'm not going down the rabbit hole today.

Thanks for the invitation, but I'm going to have to decline.

Shrug

Oh, hi, disgust!

Expansion

When we practice response prevention, the urges to compulse and the emotions compulsions aim to resolve linger. Therefore, to practice response prevention, we must improve our ability to be present with emotions and urges without attempting to change them. When it comes to accepting feelings and urges, my favorite concrete tool is the ACT skill of expansion.

The practice of expansion involves locating the individual sensations that make up emotions in your body. If you're feeling anxious, you might notice a tightening in your shoulders, throat, chest, or jaw. You might notice heaviness in your stomach, a rapid heartbeat, or shallow breathing.

Once we've noticed where a feeling exists in our body, we want to approach these sensations differently than we usually would. Typically, when people experience emotions that they don't like as well as the physical sensations that accompany them, they begin to resist them. As you've now experienced with the piece of paper exercise in chapter 6, this resistance causes more distress. So, instead of trying to force these feelings from our bodies, we want to expand to make space for them. Hence, expansion.

The invitation with expansion is to breathe into these areas of your body where you're noticing these physical sensations and imagine with each breath that you could make space for these sensations. Oftentimes, breathing exercises suggest we breathe in the good and exhale the bad. Expansion is, in some ways, the opposite of that. We're breathing in with the intention of being a kind host to all emotions. You wouldn't shove your house guest into a small corner of your home if you were trying to be kind. You wouldn't have a great relationship with that guest if you did. Instead, we want to open toward our emotions. As we breathe out, we can imagine dropping the barriers we've built against our feelings. If you'd trapped that guest in the corner, we'd want to pull down any barriers that have been keeping them there.

This exercise helps us stay with our sensory experiences, thus reducing active thinking about the sensations, which often gives way to judging. Let's walk through this exercise point by point so you can lead yourself through it when challenging emotions arise.

We'll need to have some feelings with which to practice expansion, which means we'll be doing some exposure work. If you're not willing to explore exposures yet, you can return to this exercise when an emotion occurs naturally. Keep in mind, though, that naturally occurring triggers often lead to more intense emotions and that it's harder to learn new skills when big feelings are overwhelming you. Starting with purposefully exposing yourself to smaller triggers can help you get your bearings.

To start, think of an obsession you have and condense it into a single phrase. You can use the "what if" you created in chapter 1 as a starting point. From there, you can replace the words "what if" with "maybe." For instance, if you struggle with real event OCD, you might have the thought *What if I acted immorally in that situation?* making the condensed phrase *Maybe I acted immorally in that situation.* Jot it down.

____

____

____

____

If you haven't identified a central theme of doubt in the context of your obsessions, then bring something mildly triggering to mind. Perhaps it's an image that causes disgust or that triggers the desire for symmetry.

Now set a timer for thirty seconds and repeat this phrase or focus on the image for that duration. By the end of the thirty seconds, you're likely to have some amount of distress with which to work. Give it a try.

Once you've finished building your emotion, let's shift your attention to your physical sensations. Notice where the emotion you're experiencing lives in your body. If you're not sure what physical feelings you are experiencing, you can mentally scan from the top of your head to the bottom of your feet. Imagine that your attention is like one of those laser light body scanners in a sci-fi film—you know, the kind that might beam you up? Before it transports your molecules to the far reaches of the universe, it will first need to capture information from every part of your body. That blue light would slowly trail across your forehead to the eyebrows, across your eyes, nose, cheeks, and jaw. Likewise, allow your attention to travel to these areas and consider what you feel there. You may notice a tightness in your jaw, your throat, your shoulders, your chest, or your stomach. You might notice a fast energy zooming from one body part to the next. You might notice your heart is beating faster or a weight pulling on your stomach. There's no right or wrong way to feel. Just take note of anything that stands out.

If you think you feel "normal," you're actually identifying a judgment of a feeling, not a feeling. Even if you don't think your physical sensations are different than they are typically, just take note of what you're experiencing. These sensations may be subtle, intense, or somewhere in between.

Now, pick one physical experience and imagine that there is a deflated balloon in that area of your body. As you breathe in, picture this balloon inflating. As you breathe out, soften into the experience. As you breathe in, expand this area. As you breathe out, release into the experience. As you breathe in, open, and as you breathe out, relax into the sensation. Breathing in, stretching this space, breathing out, melting into the experience.

Take a moment to consider what you're experiencing now. Are you more tense? Less? Remember, the aim here isn't to relax these areas but instead to try to expand these areas and be a gracious host to these experiences for the duration of their stay. It just so happens that this will likely support reduced resistance and thus reduce your overall tension.

Of course, you won't necessarily make actual physical space. All the same, you will be approaching your feelings from a place of curiosity and openness. This will help you drop the resistance that causes added suffering.

Notice if you've described some of these sensory experiences using the phrase "It feels like." As we've discussed, if you say, "I feel like I can't breathe," that's a lot more likely to increase distress than "I feel a pressure in my chest and my breaths are short." It's best to stick with the raw sensory experiences as sometimes comparisons create a frightening narrative.

It won't be necessary to run through this thoroughly every time you're triggered. With some practice, it'll be easier to identify physical sensations associated with emotions and to open toward them.

Misgivings About Acceptance

Now that you've been introduced to these exercises from ACT, you might be noticing some concerns crop up about acceptance. If you have, you're not alone! Most people have some misgivings about practicing acceptance. But these concerns are usually based on misunderstandings. Let's explore some common misconceptions that might stop you from practicing acceptance.

Acceptance ≠ Resignation

Acceptance is not the same as resignation. Accepting sadness does not involve resigning yourself to a permanent state of sadness but rather accepting that right now, you feel sad. You don't know what you will feel in the next minute, hour, or day. Accepting something that may not happen doesn't make sense.

Also, accepting thoughts is not the same as accepting them as truth. Acceptance involves allowing thoughts to be present. *I accept that I am having this thought that I could be lying to myself about my gender identity* is different from *I accept that I am lying about my gender identity.* We want to accept the *presence* of thoughts, not to accept their content as factual.

Acceptance ≠ Liking

Accepting the presence of something is not the same as liking something. I can accept that it is raining without liking that it is raining. You don't have to make yourself like the rain. You can even accept the awareness of your preference for sunny days while accepting the rain.

What If Acceptance Is a Mistake?

Many worry that accepting something is irresponsible. For example: *This thought that I could harm someone might be a sign. What if I accept it, and I do* harm *someone?* Remember, though: your decision to refrain from responding isn't random. In chapter 5, we used cognitive skills to determine how it makes sense to respond to obsessions, and you made a deliberate choice to accept uncertainty. We're now working to respond to our obsessions without trying to resolve them. Of course, the possibility that acceptance could be a mistake still exists. We can't get rid of possibilities. But the possibility that something could be irresponsible is not the same as accepting that the behavior is irresponsible.

I Don't Want to "Just Accept" Something

When people hear acceptance, they often think this involves becoming passive in the face of life. But acceptance and action aren't mutually exclusive. I can, for example, accept thoughts and sensations related to back pain and doubt about what that pain is, while scheduling a doctor's appointment. Given that I cannot change the thoughts and sensations, accepting their presence is the only thing that makes sense between setting and going to the appointment.

If I don't accept my back-related thoughts and sensations, I may get lost reviewing the days preceding the injury, attempting to "prove" that I'm not actually hurt. I might try to ignore the reality of my pain and, in this process, avoid seeing a doctor who could help. I might keep wishing that the pain weren't there and build frustration around the pain. I might excessively check my back pain, and, in so doing, make it more intense. In short, my resistance will add suffering to my pain, and my pain will still be there.

Ultimately, the question is not whether we should accept thoughts or feelings, but rather whether it makes sense to address them. If I've gotten a few opinions about my back and guidance about how to support myself, then it doesn't make sense to go to the doctor every time I wonder or feel doubt about my diagnosis. Instead, it makes sense to do the physical therapy that I was prescribed. Accepting thoughts and feelings helps us address genuine issues without wasting time trying to resolve thoughts and feelings about that issue.

Even when we can't take action to effect change, accepting our reality allows us to prioritize supportive actions. I can accept that I have back pain in spite of my physical therapy while simultaneously dropping rumination and practicing self-compassion. If I'm unwilling to acknowledge the reality of my pain, then I will be caught trying to explain it away and will have difficulty supporting myself through it.

Bottom line: acceptance isn't about disempowering you. Quite the contrary, accepting what we cannot change—our thoughts, emotions, urges, and sensations—frees us up to change what we can: how we treat ourselves in the face of our internal experiences.

Acceptance Is a Practice

We've now covered several mindfulness tools that can support response prevention vis-à-vis acceptance. These include:

- Cognitive defusion
- Nonengagement responses
- Expansion

Since acceptance isn't exactly an action verb with concrete steps, the "how to" of acceptance can seem like a tricky business. Hopefully you can see how the practices of defusion and expansion function as a "how to" by offering specific skills to support you in dropping resistance. By setting our minds about the task of nonjudgmentally witnessing our present moment experiences, we are no longer resisting these experiences.

It's normal to weave in and out of acceptance. Since remaining in acceptance is so challenging, our focus is on how to pivot back toward acceptance when we notice resistance. We might view acceptance as a two-part practice to support us in consistently pivoting. The "first part," the part we've been discussing, involves dropping resistance. Defusion, nonengagement responses, and expansion are all about dropping resistance. When using these practices, we stop trying to make thoughts and feelings go away and instead settle into nonjudgmental awareness. When we do this, we also drop any active comparison about how much better life would be if our thoughts and feelings were different.

The second part of acceptance is in the choice to drop resistance over and over again. While it would be wonderful if we could say *I accept this* once and permanently be in this accepting state, that's just not how human brains work. You can resolve to accept something and then, shortly afterward, start resisting it again. If I accept that I have a mosquito bite and then moments later I start thinking about how unfair it is that I got bit by the mosquito, I'm no longer accepting the mosquito bite. Likewise, if I accept the presence of thoughts about the "rightness" of my relationship, noticing them without judgment, then I start ruminating about how awful the thoughts are and how much I wish they would just get out of my head, then I am no longer accepting them. To develop peaceful coexistence with our thoughts and feelings, we have to commit to repeatedly dropping resistance. We have to repeatedly drop mental compulsions.

Think of it this way: to end the war with your internal experiences, you need both a short-term truce and a long-term peace treaty. If I call a ceasefire and then resume battle, then I'm still at war. If I lay down my weapons and commit to continue setting them aside, then I am no longer at war. Of course, in this analogy, we may pick up our "weapons," or resistance and mental compulsions, again without even realizing that we have. If you've done this, do not fret! The "treaty" in recovery involves noticing when we're starting to fight again and dropping the fight as quickly as we can manage.

Now that we've covered some practices that help with dropping resistance and supporting acceptance, let's turn toward mindfulness exercises that support both reorientation toward the present moment and the maintenance of acceptance.

Chapter 8

Mindfulness Skills for Shifting Attention

I often hear people say, "Acceptance didn't work!" Usually what they mean is that acceptance didn't get rid of their internal experiences. Translation: after initially accepting an experience, they began to resist it again. Resistance is, well, hard to resist. We often return to resistance without realizing it.

One of the best ways to refrain from reengaging in resistance and related unhelpful mental behaviors is to refocus on something else. Idle minds are mental compulsions' playground. It is clearer to see the importance of refocusing when we consider response prevention with physical compulsions. If someone who washes compulsively turns off the faucet after a single, time-limited wash, this in and of itself is technically response prevention. But if that person stands there staring at the faucet, they're much more likely to turn it back on and perform that washing ritual that they initially avoided. Besides, staring at the sink isn't much of a life. If you were practicing response prevention in this context, you would walk away from the sink and get back to living.

Likewise, if you want to stop engaging in mental behaviors, dropping that behavior is unlikely to be enough. While we can't walk away from our brains, we can learn to redirect them. Through mindfulness practices, like meditation, you can learn to resettle your attention on the present, helping you to drop the thinking and reengage with what's meaningful to you.

Mindfulness aims to train our so-called "monkey mind," or our minds' natural tendency to chatter and wander. Minds say all sorts of things and amble all over. As you're going about your day, you might find yourself planning or daydreaming. You could also find yourself listing off your mistakes, berating yourself for a choice you made, ruminating, worrying, or performing some form of mental compulsion. This wandering is not an issue. The practice of mindfulness helps us to get better at nonjudgmentally noticing when our monkey mind starts wandering. And when we notice, *Oh look, I'm thinking*, we can reorient toward the present.

Shifting attention is not the same as distracting yourself to avoid having thoughts. Such distraction is a form of resistance. Refocusing attention involves allowing for automatic thoughts to arise while attending to activities that matter more to you than mental compulsions.

Let's say you have existential OCD and you're at work when you start having obsessions about whether you're living in a simulation. You might start checking your feelings to determine whether you "feel real." When you notice this checking, you can nonjudgmentally acknowledge "thinking" and, if being a reliable worker is more important to you than checking your feelings, you can refocus your attention on your work.

We want you to do what you would do were it not for the presence of your internal experiences. If you weren't anxious, would you refocus your attention on the book you're reading? If you weren't having these thoughts, would you go on a walk? The most important part of response prevention is getting you back to living your life on your terms.

With that said, let's discuss some practices that can help you on this leg of the journey.

Daily Mindfulness Exercises

To hone your mindfulness skills, pick a daily activity that you perform anyway and commit to approaching it with mindfulness. You might brush your teeth, wash dishes, cook, eat, or walk mindfully. This daily mindfulness exercise ties mindfulness practice to a routine or habit that has already been established, thus making it less challenging to prioritize and easier to remember.

As you practice, you will anchor your attention in the sensory experiences related to the activity. You might focus on sights, sounds, smells, tastes, and physical sensations. Resting your attention on your sensory experience is a way of connecting to the present. When you wander, whether into compulsions or more neutral forms of thinking, you can acknowledge this nonjudgmentally and gently reorient to the present.

Let's illustrate by using the example of brushing your teeth. If you were brushing your teeth as your daily mindfulness exercise, you may taste or smell the toothpaste. You can recognize the difference in the flavor as the toothpaste spreads across different parts of your tongue. You can notice if the scent is sweet, spicy, or some combination. You might hear the whir of a motor if you use an electric toothbrush, and you could listen to the sounds of the bristles against your teeth. You likely feel the brush against your gums and tongue. You might see a faucet or sink in front of you or your reflection in the mirror.

While noticing your sensory experience, we want you to do your utmost to refrain from judging the experience. You might hate the whir of the motor or love the taste of the toothpaste. You might feel refreshed or annoyed by the process. Whatever comes up for you, do your best to approach it with curiosity.

Sometime in this process of noticing, your mind will wander. You may be planning your next meal or mentally arguing with your boss about something. You might start trying to get certainty about your latest obsession. Noticing this, nonjudgmentally, is a moment of mindfulness. This might sound like *Oh, look, I'm thinking*. Be careful not to give way to berating yourself for getting lost in thinking. It's a normal part of this process.

Once you have noticed that your mind has wandered, you have the opportunity to bring your attention back to what's happening here and now. In this exercise, that looks like grounding in the sensory experiences associated with toothbrushing. You may find yourself thinking many times over the course of one toothbrushing session. That's normal! This noticing allows us to build our capacity to identify and disengage from mental compulsions.

Practicing mindfulness purposefully in this way can help us call upon this skill of returning to the present moment when we get caught in mental compulsions. Having a greater capacity to shift our attention will allow us to be more present in our lives.

Daily Mindfulness Exercise

Choose a daily activity to practice with mindfulness. Now let's do a trial run! Bring this book along with you while you perform the activity you've chosen so that you can write down some notes. Taking the time to walk through this step by step will help you practice the task mindfully during your daily routine.

To start, consider if you notice any smells. Practice using nonjudgmental language as you describe the experience. Is the scent earthy? Sweet? Sour? Salty?

____

____

If you find yourself trying to figure out what's causing the smell, come back to the embodied experience of smelling. For example, focus on inhaling the sweetness in the air rather than on labeling the smell as chocolate chip cookies. Don't worry if the word "cookies" pops into your head, though. Our brains are association-making machines, so this is bound to happen. We just want to prioritize the embodied experience of smelling over the analysis of the smell.

If you notice yourself saying, "I like that smell" or "Yuck, that smell is gross," try to reorient toward noticing the smell. The emphasis here is on experiencing the smell rather than actively evaluating it. That said, if you do notice you've judged the smell, can you notice your judgments nonjudgmentally? "Oh look, I'm really resisting that experience!"

Now check in with yourself about what you see, again using nonjudgmental language. Consider using shapes, colors, and textures to describe what you see so that you are more in touch with the raw sensory experience rather than your interpretation of it.

____

____

Do you hear anything? If so, what sounds do you hear? Try to be descriptive and play with the idea of separating the sounds from what you believe to be causing the sounds. This will help you engage in listening rather than thinking about what you're hearing.

____

____

Is touch part of this experience? If so, consider what you can feel physically in association with the activity. Notice the textures and sensations. Is it rough or smooth? Slick or sticky? Again, when you're engaged in the activity, you needn't describe these experiences verbally. You can just notice the physical experience of the different sensations occurring.

____

____

What can you taste? Does the taste change over time? If you are eating something, you might recognize the textures against your tongue, gums, lips, and mouth as well as the sweetness or saltiness. Again, if positive or negative associations arise, notice them nonjudgmentally.

____

____

Now that you have a clear sense of this experience, put a note up in the area associated with that activity (such as near your shoes if you're going to take a mindful walk). While the entirety of the activity needn't be done mindfully, try to spend at least a few minutes in this practice per day. The more you practice, the easier it will become.

Meditation

There are many types of meditation, but we'll be discussing focused-attention meditation. As with the daily mindfulness activity, the aim with focused-attention meditation is to "anchor" in the present moment. Instead of anchoring in the sensory experience of an activity, meditation often instructs individuals to ground their attention in their felt experience of breathing. While I will use breathing in the instructions that follow, you can use the sensory experience of hearing sounds if that's easier for you.

When your mind wanders in meditation, you practice noticing what's happening in a nonjudgmental and thus accepting way. You then reorient your attention toward your anchor. Thus this skill can help us access an alternative to endlessly thinking: an alternative to mental compulsions.

The breath is a reliably accessible present moment experience. Since the present moment is where most of life exists, tuning into the present means tuning into life. What's more, the breath isn't particularly stimulating, which is actually helpful for our purposes. It makes it more likely that your attention will wander and offers more opportunities to practice reorienting.

Focused-attention meditation is like a form of exercise for your mind. Metaphorically speaking, people who mentally compulse have an imbalance in their mental musculature. Over time, they've strengthened the muscles of excessive analysis, leaving their disengage-and-reorient muscles to atrophy from underuse. They need the mental equivalent of physical therapy to correct this imbalance, and meditation is the ideal PT for supporting response prevention. Noticing internal experiences, without judgment, builds our nonjudgment muscle while refocusing on the present builds our shifting-attention muscle.

When you begin meditating, you may think you're bad at it because your mind is wandering. But your mind *will* wander—a lot. This is normal. The goal isn't to stop your mind from wandering but to catch it and bring it back when it does.

Meditation isn't a relaxation exercise but rather an exercise intended to train your mind. So, if you feel different feelings while meditating, which you are likely to do, remember that feelings don't speak to the quality of meditation. The goal isn't to make yourself feel a certain way but to witness the states that arise, nonjudgmentally.

Reading about these concepts will only get you so far. So, let's practice!

A Basic Focused-Attention Mindfulness Meditation

Yes, meditation can sound intimidating, but it's actually simple! Read through these instructions and then give it a try yourself. You can also download an audio recording of this exercise to listen to and follow along:

1. Sit in an upright posture. You needn't be overly rigid or tense but do your best to avoid slouching and keep alert.

2. Close your eyes if you're willing as it's easier to focus on the exercise with fewer distractions competing for your attention. Otherwise, allow your eyes to gaze downward in an unfocused manner.

3. Start by taking a few deep breaths just to get settled into this experience. In through the nose and out through the mouth.

4. Now, let your breath fall into its natural rhythm. You don't need to control the breath or follow a pattern; just watch what your breath does and explore how it feels. Focus on the embodied experience of the breath rather than thinking about the breath.

5. As you watch your breath, you might notice the sounds associated with your breathing, the feeling of expansion and contraction in your chest, and the quality of the breath against your

nostrils. The aim is to get curious about the experience of breathing. Notice any thinking about your breathing and do your best to orient toward the embodied experience.

6. Before too long, you'll notice that your mind has wandered. How do I know this? Because this is what minds do! If you've caught your mind wandering, notice this without judgment. You might even gently label it as "thinking." Then, reorient your attention to your experience of breathing in the present moment.

7. Continue on like this for several minutes (set a timer and aim for at least 3–5). Rest your attention on your breath, nonjudgmentally notice when your attention has been pulled away, and gently reorient toward the study of the breath.

Focused Attention Meditation Debrief

Once you're done with that 3–5-minute exercise, let's debrief. You can also download and print copies of these debrief questions at http://www.newharbinger.com/55541.

What was this experience like for you? What did you notice?

____

____

____

Were you able to prioritize the practice of nonjudgment? Was that challenging or easy?

____

____

Are you judging your performance as "good" or "bad"? Based on what?

____

____

Did you wander more or less than you anticipated that you would?

____

____

Were you surprised by any part of the experience?

Just as with the daily mindfulness activity, meditation allows us to practice dropping resistance toward our experiences and reorienting our attention toward the present. We're flexing the muscle that will allow us to:

1. notice thoughts, feelings, and mental compulsions, nonjudgmentally
2. drop resistance of thoughts and feelings that leads to mental compulsions
3. reorient toward what matters in the present moment

Self-Compassion Practice

While self-compassion isn't a mindfulness practice per se, mindfulness is central to exercising self-compassion. Self-compassion can help us interrupt mental compulsions and therefore support response prevention. It can also offer a new focal point for our attention, thus reducing the likelihood that we will return to mental compulsions. Kristin Neff and Christopher Germer have written extensively about self-compassion and have broken the concept down into three basic steps (Neff and Germer 2018).

Mindfulness

We start by nonjudgmentally noting our present-moment experience. We can use the skills we're developing, including nonengagement responses and defusion, to reflect what we're seeing. For example: *Oh look, I'm having the thought that I could go to hell.* Or *I'm noticing that I'm feeling anxious.*

Common Humanity

Oftentimes, we assume that we are alone in difficult experiences. With just over eight billion people on the planet, though, it's exceedingly unlikely that we are alone in any experience. And recognizing that we are not alone can be of great comfort and strengthen our resolve to forge onward when challenges arise.

To reflect on common humanity, you can complete the sentence: "I bet a lot of people…" This might sound like "I bet a lot of people have fears about their salvation." Or "I bet a lot of people feel anxious after thoughts like that."

Side bonus: Recognizing common humanity can promote acceptance. When we acknowledge how universal our experience is, we're less apt to fight it.

Self-Kindness

This third step involves talking to yourself as you would a cherished friend. While those who mentally compulse spend a lot of time in their heads, their inner dialogue is rarely kind, and thus self-kindness can be an uncomfortable undertaking. But just because something is uncomfortable doesn't mean it's disingenuous or wrong. We tend to feel comfortable with what is familiar to us, and thus comfort can indicate that we'd be better served doing something else.

So, what does self-kindness sound like? You can use phrases that you find comforting as a starting point. Consider words that help you tap into a sense of warmth and gentleness. For instance, you could use the phrase "my love" to generate that sense of kindness toward yourself. You might say, *Oh my love, I can see how painful this is for you. I've got you. I'll hold your hand, and we'll walk through this together.* I can completely appreciate how strange this might sound. But try it out. Or try something else out. Consider what you would say to a friend who was faced with challenging emotions. Maybe something like *I'm here for you. We can hold this.*

You might wonder if being kind means allowing yourself to do compulsions. But kindness and permissiveness are not one and the same. In fact, when you know how compulsions are likely to impact you, the choice to compulse is anything but kind. In contrast, the choice to refrain from mental compulsions is an expression of self-kindness. It may be uncomfortable in the short term, but in the long run, it supports our ability to engage in our lives and promotes well-being. Indeed, response prevention is both firm and kind, thus reflecting the practice of compassionate accountability.

Committing to dropping self-flagellation is also an expression of self-kindness. You wouldn't expect your relationship to someone else to thrive if you were constantly putting them down. Likewise, beating up on yourself will likely result in a pretty poor relationship with yourself.

In addition to considering how you speak to yourself, you can use touch to express self-kindness, too. Maybe that involves wrapping yourself in a blanket, putting your hand over your heart, or stroking your arm. When in doubt, consider how you would show someone else tenderness and go from there.

Summing Up Self-Compassion

If you have a tough time practicing self-compassion, you can come back to these three pillars to support you in expressing compassion toward yourself. For example:

Mindfulness: *I'm noticing that I'm having a strong feeling of distress and I really want to do a compulsion.*

Common humanity: *I bet a lot of people with OCD find they want to do compulsions when they're distressed.*

Self-kindness: *It's important to me that I support myself and the life I want to live, so I'm going to hold myself as I make space for distress. I've got this!*

The expression of self-compassion supports you in traversing scary territories—the kind of terrain that pops up when we refrain from compulsions. In this way it is a great tool for supporting response prevention. It also has the fringe benefit of supporting a kind and healthy relationship with yourself.

Bringing It All Together

In this chapter, we've covered several additional mindfulness tools that support response prevention by promoting acceptance *and* helping us practice refocusing our attention. These include:

- daily mindfulness activities
- focused-attention meditation
- self-compassion

You've likely spent years and years resisting certain thoughts and feelings—especially obsessions, anxiety, guilt, disgust, and discomfort—that you've found to be unpleasant. Thus resistance is a deeply ingrained behavioral response to these internal experiences. When practiced regularly, the mindfulness we've explored in this chapter will help you better practice nonjudgment, drop resistance, and shift your attention.

Essentially, you're learning to drop the act of thinking. This is critical given that disengaging from thinking is the essence of dropping mental compulsions. When you're mentally compulsing, you can notice that you're lost in thinking and bring your attention back to whatever is happening in the here and now. As with meditation, you will have to do this repeatedly. But every time you practice, you get better at noticing internal experiences and reorienting your attention. One moment at a time, you get to be present to your life! We're getting your life back!

Imagine for a moment that your attention is a spotlight and your mind is a stage. You might notice that your attention has wandered much like a runaway spotlight could. Your attention may land on thoughts that are unimportant to you—the equivalent of the spotlight settling on a random box on the stage.

You don't need to explode the random box, push it off the stage, or get someone to carry it off. The box isn't a problem: the fact that it's getting all your attention is the problem. And detonating the box or pushing it off the stage would give it *more* attention. So, when your spotlight wanders, you can simply redirect it toward what is important to you. The spotlight isn't bad for wandering, nor is your attention—that's just their nature. The only thing you have agency over is what you do with this reality. Do you try to get rid of the box even though these attempts won't work and will detract from the main action of your play? Or do you simply keep bringing the spotlight back to the focal point that matters to you?

Now that we have the skills needed to bring the spotlight back to the focal point that matters most to us, we can more effectively disengage from mental compulsions in the face of exposures. In chapter 10, we'll use exposure and response prevention to create scenarios that lead us to focus on that random box more frequently and intently. This will give us the chance to practice bringing the spotlight back to what matters to us. By practicing, we'll get better at shifting that spotlight back just as quickly as we can whenever that spotlight is stuck on that box.

Before we dive into exposure and response prevention, chapter 9 will consider one more strategy that can support you in sidestepping mental compulsions.

Chapter 9

Cognitive-Behavioral Tools for Response Prevention

In chapter 5, we learned to use cognitive tools to assess what mental behaviors are irrational, unhelpful, and in conflict with our values. We did this to foster your willingness to disengage from mental compulsions. We then covered mindfulness skills to support you in practicing acceptance and reorienting to the present whenever you determine that thinking doesn't make sense. But what do you do when you determine *some* thinking makes sense? Before we discuss exposures, we'll cover one more response prevention skill to support you in reorienting away from mental compulsions: the skill of helpful thinking.

Helpful Thinking That Complements Acceptance

Just because mental compulsions involve resistance doesn't mean all thinking is at odds with acceptance. There are helpful ways to think just as there are helpful behaviors that can occur alongside acceptance.

Yes, some thinking can be summarily rejected as both unimportant and unhelpful. But sometimes our thoughts, or at least some component of our thoughts, do deserve *some* attention. Navigating thinking without giving way to resistance and excessive analysis or rumination can be tricky! In these instances, we want to consider what *type* of thinking best serves us so we can shift out of unhelpful modes of thinking in favor of helpful approaches.

Enter rumination-focused cognitive behavioral therapy (RF-CBT), developed by Ed Watkins and explored at length in his 2016 book *Rumination-Focused Cognitive-Behavioral Therapy for Depression*. Studies have shown that RF-CBT is a promising approach for reducing rumination and depressive symptoms (Li and Tang 2024) and addressing symptoms of anxiety (Tulbure et al. 2025; Joubert et al. 2023). Thus, it has clear application for those struggling with mental compulsions.

Let's consider ideas from and inspired by this approach to help you disengage from rumination.

Abstract vs. Concrete Thinking in RF-CBT

Abstract processing plays a crucial role in ruminative thinking. You're more likely to get stuck while thinking abstractly, or trying to answer questions about the meaning and significance of an event, than you are while thinking concretely, or considering how you plan to respond to the same event. You're also more likely to get stuck if you overgeneralize about circumstances than if you're specific about a particular event.

Since our thinking style is so impactful, identifying abstract thinking patterns and reorienting toward a concrete processing style can be beneficial. To do so, we need to understand the difference between "why-type" and "how" questions. Why-type questions aim to address the relevance or meaning of an experience. With OCD, such questions often sound like "Why did I have that thought?" or "What does this feeling mean?" The endless digging central to why-type thinking is at odds with acceptance.

"How" questions aim to determine how we want to show up as things are and support the development of concrete steps. They might sound like "How can I move forward given the presence of this thought?" or "What steps do I want to take to address this situation?" When we consider obsessions concretely, we can (1) determine if there is something to be done and then address it or (2) find that there isn't a problem to be solved and get back to living life.

Seeing that not all why-type questions start with "why" and not all how questions start with "how," some might find that differentiating between philosophizing and problem-solving is more intuitive. For someone with harm OCD, philosophizing or why-type questions might sound like:

> *What does it mean that I felt angry when that image popped into my mind? Maybe that means something about my character. Perhaps I could hurt someone. Would someone who didn't want to hurt someone experience anger when they saw that image? No, they'd probably experience disgust…*

As you can see, philosophizing involves broad questions and aims to interpret events. It takes specific experiences and tries to generalize them. This type of thinking invariably results in more thinking because there aren't definitive answers to these questions. In the example above, we can recognize that an image and emotion could indicate lots of different things: a vivid imagination, an emotional sensitivity, that you are a human being who feels emotions, or that someone was acting in a way that you found to be frustrating. Of course, the "maybe" that the harm OCD sufferer focuses on is the potential that it could indicate a murderous urge. Is this one of any number of possibilities? I suppose it is. But no amount of thinking is going to lead to a definitive answer about what the image and emotion mean. Philosophizing is never-ending and keeps us trapped in our own minds!

While philosophizing widens the scope of a single circumstance, problem-solving narrows things down. Problem-solving might sound like:

> *I felt angry when that image appeared in my mind as I was sitting on the couch next to my sister. I felt scared about having that thought and feeling. Given that I can't control thoughts and feelings, I won't*

try to change those. I will, however, consider how I want to show up in this present moment. Do I want to get up and walk away from my sister because of my fear, or do I want to stay and watch this movie with her? How can I behave in a way that reflects the kind of person that I want to be right now?

You'll notice that problem-solving is more specific. That's because we are trying to determine how it makes sense to show up in a particular context given the facts. Indeed, context is crucial when it comes to concrete thinking (Watkins 2011). Thus, getting clear about the specifics of what's happening in this moment can guide you back to more helpful thinking.

You may also notice that while philosophizing is nebulous and broad, problem-solving is tangible and action-oriented. Problem-solving is a form of thinking that results in action rather than more thinking. Once the person in the above example decides how they want to behave, the next step is to put that plan into action.

So, philosophizing can sound like:

- Why did that happen?
- What does this mean?
- What will happen because of this?

Problem-solving questions can include:

- Is there anything to be done about this?
- How can I approach this situation?
- What can I change about this situation?
- What can I do in this situation to get me closer to my values?

Some ways to differentiate between the two include:

Problem-solving	Philosophizing
Specific	Broad
Present-oriented	Past and future-oriented
Action-oriented	Focused on meaning making

Now consider the OCD-related questions you try to resolve. If you have existential OCD, you may ask yourself if you're living your life correctly. If you have self-harm obsessions, you may ask yourself whether you are capable of taking your own life. Jot down your questions in the space provided.

____

____

____

____

Consider how you typically respond to these questions. Do you try to answer these broad questions in black and white ways? Do you arrive at answers? Are they satisfying? Do you find yourself returning to the same questions over and over? Is philosophizing involved in your habitual response? Write your answers in the space provided.

____

____

____

____

Now consider how you would approach this question using a concrete, problem-solving lens. For example, if you ask, "Am I in the right relationship?" you might consider whether there's anything you would like to do now in these particular circumstances to address any specific challenge that has come up. Would you like to communicate something to your partner? If the answer is yes, then how would you like to communicate it? If the answer is no, then how do you want to show up in this moment? Do you want to continue to think about this question? Share your reflections in the space provided.

____

____

____

____

There is absolutely nothing wrong with philosophizing, but when there's an imbalance between abstract and concrete thinking, we are likely to veer into more and more thinking. For those trying to break free from mental compulsions, learning how to reorient toward concrete thinking can promote flexibility and support your ability to actively think on your own terms.

Chapter 10

Practicing Exposure and Response Prevention

It's time to put our new response prevention skills to the test by adding exposures into the mix and thus learning to face triggers *without* mentally compulsing.

While this book has focused on mental compulsions, it's not uncommon for people who perform mental compulsions to perform observable compulsions, too. If this is you, remember that all compulsions, by definition, interfere with our ability to live life on our terms. Given this, we want to practice response prevention for all types of compulsions, not just the mental ones. Let's briefly cover some common forms of compulsions to help you clarify which behaviors to target with response prevention.

Other Forms of Compulsions

Just as many with OCD reassure themselves that they are safe, many excessively seek reassurance from others. Someone with relationship OCD might ask others what they think about their relationship. They might ask every time new relationship-related anxiety arises or about one triggering instance over and over. They might ask the same question repeatedly to the same person until it feels "right" or ask many different people.

If you find that you ask people questions repeatedly to gain certainty, you may notice that this puts a strain on your relationship with the reassurer because the relentless attempts to resolve anxiety can interfere with meaningful connections.

One way or another, excessive reassurance seeking, like excessive thinking, impairs your ability to live life on your terms. Therefore, we want to practice disengaging from reassurance seeking when triggered.

You might also engage in overt behavioral compulsions. For example, you might wash, check, or order objects excessively to rid yourself of discomfort, anxiety, and doubt. If these behaviors interfere with your overall well-being, then response prevention will also involve reducing or refraining from these behaviors.

No matter the type of compulsion, we can use the same tools outlined in the preceding chapters to support us in accepting emotions, reorienting toward the present, and centering our values. While space prevents me from providing an in-depth exploration of all compulsions, there are many other wonderful resources that talk about compulsions more generally. If you think you'd benefit from more information, check out Jon Hershfield and Tom Corboy's *The Mindfulness Workbook for OCD*.

Avoidance

Avoidance is another problematic behavior in the context of OCD. While response prevention addresses the various compulsions people perform after being triggered, exposures directly tackle the *avoidance* of triggers. Avoidance can have a profoundly limiting impact on life and can be every bit as disruptive as overt and covert compulsions. Someone with sexual orientation OCD might avoid spending time with specific triggering friends, even if these friendships are meaningful to them. People with postpartum obsessions might avoid their baby even though they care deeply about being present for their little one.

The Practice of ERP

As we begin this work, remember the goal is to get better at feeling your feelings rather than to feel less. We are strengthening your capacity to feel so that you stop mentally compulsing. Such strengthening requires practice, which is why we step into situations that are likely to cause anxiety and discomfort. Active exposures afford us opportunities to practice responding to emotions differently.

Just as muscles build with each weightlifting rep, your capacity to drop mental compulsions increases every time you disengage. Taking it one rep at a time and increasing the difficulty gradually makes progress sustainable. You don't build muscle by rushing to lift the heaviest weight, and you won't build your capacity by rushing to face the most intense trigger. Pushing yourself past the edge will just lead to the mental equivalent of pulling a muscle—you'll probably do a bunch of compulsions and might be completely put off from doing exposures in the future.

Imagine that you're training for a marathon. Going from couch to 26.2 miles without any training sounds like a recipe for injury, right? Slow and steady is the name of the game when it comes to marathon training and cultivating your willingness to feel. There is no rush, because there isn't really an end to the journey. You may meet a goal like running a certain number of miles or facing a specific trigger. Ultimately, though, we want to increase your strength, not outrun fear.

White knuckling through your distress misses the point. If you grit your teeth through your fear, you're increasing resistance and creating suffering. With ERP, attitude is everything. By drawing on our mindfulness skills from the preceding chapters, we can approach distress with the intention of making space and opening toward these emotions.

You deserve serious kudos for getting to this point. Misconceptions about ERP sometimes prevent people from getting on the path to recovery. You've got this, one step at a time. Now, let's discuss different types of exposures.

Incidental Exposures

Exposures are everywhere. In fact, trigger is just another word for exposure. Let's say that you're struggling with sensorimotor OCD, and your primary obsession is related to your awareness of your breath. You can't get away from your breath. In fact, breathing is guaranteed to happen all day, every day. Triggers are inescapable, and this really could be said for any subtype.

We know, now, that mental compulsions themselves are the problem even if they're masquerading as the solution. So, if you're already doing the hard work of facing your fears, let's stop throwing salt in the wound with those mental compulsions! If given the chance, you might as well practice responding to them differently. After all, every time you practice responding differently, it becomes easier to respond differently.

Looking for Exposure Opportunities

Let's consider triggers that arise in your everyday life to help you identify opportunities to practice response prevention.

To start, review the last 3–5 days. As you scan through each day, think back to moments when you felt anxious or uncomfortable. For each of those moments, consider what happened just before your anxiety or discomfort spiked. Maybe you noticed a car drive by and remembered your hit-and-run fears. Maybe you thought about a friend and the thought led to concerns that you could have yelled an obscenity at them.

Jot down the situations in the space provided:

____

____

____

____

____

____

Now that you've practiced identifying triggers, you'll catch them more quickly in daily life and be better prepared to practice response prevention.

Now think about any times you found yourself stuck in analysis, rumination, or some other form of mental compulsion. If you need help identifying your mental compulsions, reference the list outlined in chapter one.

Also, consider any additional compulsions that you may have performed like reassurance seeking or washing your hands. Write them in the space provided.

____

____

____

____

____

These are the specific behaviors you'll want to refrain from after you've faced a trigger. You may be engaging in other compulsions that you didn't think to list here. This list is meant to pique your awareness so that you can recognize the choice to disengage.

If you had difficulty seeing your triggers or compulsions in hindsight, you can keep track of them for the coming 3–5 days. Whenever you're feeling anxious, distressed, or want to perform compulsions, consider what just happened and note these triggers and compulsions, too.

The Exposure Mindset

Now that we have a sense of your triggers, we want to shift your attitude toward them. Instead of running in the other direction and tensing at the first hint of anxiety or discomfort, the focus here is on doing things that will make us proud of ourselves.

You may have heard of a growth mindset: a person's choice to look for the ways in which a situation can help them to grow and learn. Here we will be talking about a similar idea: an exposure mindset. This is the equivalent of a growth mindset for OCD recovery. Essentially, an exposure mindset sees every trigger as an opportunity to practice feeling our feelings, reduce compulsions, and get our lives back.

With an exposure mindset, we're no longer fixated on minimizing fear. This only makes our world smaller. We're focused on cultivating our capacity and expanding our world. Instead of running away from a "bad" feeling, we're running toward fear AND toward the things that matter most.

In facing our fears head-on, we expand too. Meeting fear with a "bring it on!" attitude and making the active choice to run toward what matters to you is incredibly empowering! So, say goodbye to tiptoeing around, trying to avoid anxiety and distress. We want to get big and brazen in the face of fear and discomfort. Enter a little something that I like to call "bravehearting."

Bravehearting

Bravehearting is a verb that I made up. The origins of this verb date back to the thirteenth century and a Scottish lad by the name of William Wallace. Wallace led the rebellion against English invaders and fought for the Scots' independence.

But I want to be totally real with you. My term bravehearting was actually inspired by the 1990s Mel Gibson version of William Wallace as depicted in the blockbuster hit *Braveheart*. If you're not familiar, I encourage you to look up the film. When you do, you'll likely see a photo of Mel Gibson with his blue-and-white painted face fashioned into some heroic visage running headlong into battle.

The character, and the real-life Wallace, probably felt a lot of fear. You'd have to if you were paying attention! The Scots were outnumbered. Even so, Wallace brought ferocity and conviction to battle. He went toward the fray because he wanted freedom. That's what mattered to him.

And so, I present to dictionaries the world over, my favorite verb:

braveheart (verb) /ˈbreɪvhɑːt/

a : to run toward uncomfortable emotions when they lie in the path of what matters to you.

b : to dig deep within your belly and get fired up about running toward fear and discomfort.

c : to celebrate the choice to look anxiety and distress square in the face and to do what you please

Channeling your inner Braveheart can help you build a new relationship with your feelings—one in which you're the boss. Ultimately, this metaphor isn't intended to promote an adversarial and antagonistic relationship with emotions. As we've said, feelings are not the enemy. Wallace didn't push fear away; he embraced it and, in so doing, alchemized it into courage.

Finding Your "Braveheart"

While I've gotten a lot of mileage out of bravehearting, I can appreciate that it might not be everyone's cup of tea. So now it's your turn to create your exposure mindset verb.

Consider the bravest character you've ever come across. Maybe it's Bilbo Baggins. Perhaps it's Luke Skywalker or Rey? It could even be someone you know.

Whoever you land on, consider what qualities they've brought to their own battles. Did they forge onward in the face of doubt? Can you picture them taking on their struggles? Were they willing to feel discomfort in the service of the life they wanted to live? The next time you're faced with a trigger, take a moment to tap into your own Braveheart. Bring this champion with you into the challenges you face. And please create your own verb out of the name. I'm hoping to meet one of you one day who decides that Bilboing helps you take on your exposures.

Maybe Statements

Please note that this is an advanced exercise intended to up the ante. If this gets you to a level of fear you are not yet willing to undertake, save it for another time.

When faced with doubt-inducing incidental exposures, we can also turn up the volume on anxiety to help strengthen our response prevention. Enter "maybe statements."

The approach harnesses the power of the word "maybe." As we've discussed at length, doubt is often central to the experience of OCD. People do compulsions to get rid of anxiety and discomfort, and oftentimes they achieve this by trying to resolve uncertainty. As a result, "maybe" is often OCD sufferers' kryptonite.

If your brain presents you with a "what if," it's essentially saying, "Maybe some terrible thing will happen." Your typical response has been to fight with this maybe. But if you meet maybe with maybe, you are effectively ending the argument.

To demonstrate, consider the person with existential OCD who is afraid they are unknowingly dead. They may experience derealization and have thoughts like *What if this is the afterlife?* From there, they might try to figure out if they're alive to get rid of the anxiety about a maybe—*Maybe I'm dead.* If they respond with, *Maybe*, they are acknowledging the possibility that would otherwise lead them to perform compulsions.

Yes, "maybe" is scary. That said, it's our unwillingness to acknowledge possibilities that keeps us stuck. So, saying "maybe" can help us find freedom in the face of anxiety. From there, we can use expansion or self-compassion to support us in the face of our feelings.

Summing Up Incidental Exposures

When faced with triggers "out in the wild," we want to marry an attitude of acceptance with that exposure mindset we discussed. When we see triggers, we want to practice moving toward them rather than retreating. As we approach, we want to open toward whatever feelings come up and notice whatever thoughts arise nonjudgmentally. In doing so, we are empowering ourselves and doing things that will ultimately make us proud. We're refraining from compulsions and getting our lives back!

While this attitude is the foundation of incidental exposures, it is also integral to intentional exposures. With that in mind, let's explore how to manufacture exposures so we can build our capacity to accept feelings.

Intentional Exposures

If you've read up until this page and completed the workbook exercises, then you've already done intentional exposures. In chapter 7's expansion exercise, you took a "what if" thought and created a maybe statement. You then repeated this phrase to get your uncomfortable emotions revved up. This is intentional exposure.

Traditionally, the process involves making a list—also known as a hierarchy. Your hierarchy includes things you've avoided. For instance, if you have relationship OCD, you may avoid spending time with couples who trigger anxiety. If you have false memory OCD, you may avoid places you associate with the false memory. Hanging with that couple and going to that place are exposures. List the situations, people, and places that you avoid. If your list is longer than this space will accommodate, grab an extra piece of paper.

Given that avoiding experiences makes life smaller, gradually reintroducing things you've actively avoided is one of the great benefits of intentional exposure work. Ultimately, this work paves the way to a fuller life.

Sometimes people with OCD avoid, and sometimes they continue about their lives while doing a lot of compulsions to address their distress. Earlier in this chapter, we created a list of triggers that occurred just before you started mentally compulsing over a 3–5 day span. These triggers are all possible exposures. Using these triggers as a starting point, reflect on what triggers your urge to mentally compulse (or compulse generally). Write your triggers here:

____

____

____

____

____

____

____

____

____

____

____

____

Organizing Your Hierarchy

Now that you have a list of all your triggers, let's organize it into a game plan. As you go through the list, you'll realize some triggers aren't directly replicable. For example, if you have relationship OCD and getting married is a trigger, you're probably not going to get married multiple times or get married solely for the purposes of exposure.

We would, in theory, term such an exposure *in vivo*—that is an exposure that involves doing something actively in the "real world." Since in vivo exposure isn't always a viable option, we use *imaginal* exposure to face triggers that are difficult to replicate. Instead of undertaking something in the "real world," imaginal exposures involve using the imagination as a trigger.

Imaginal Exposures

There are several different approaches to imaginal exposure work. I often start with triggering words and phrases. The person with relationship OCD might write the words "marriage" or "forever" in a place they see regularly or set timers on their phone to remind them of these words.

From there, they might progress to triggering phrases. For example, people with relationship OCD often find certain concepts to be anxiety-provoking. The notion of finding "the one" or the idea that you "just know" when someone is right for you might make them want to analyze their relationship. In this case, phrases like "I just knew" or "He's the one" could be exposures. Posting these phrases in a location, setting reminders, or even committing to using them in conversation could be useful intentional exposures.

Oftentimes, people will write triggering stories, called imaginal scripts. These scripts detail triggering scenarios that elicit fear or distress. There are several ways to write a script. Some suggest that scripts be written in the present tense, as though a distressing experience or feared outcome is happening here and now. For someone with relationship OCD, this could sound something like the following:

"It's my wedding day. I wake up feeling anxious. I try to brush it off, though the anxiety continues to build as I get dressed and head to the venue. On the drive, I realize I can't go through with this. I have to call off the wedding. I get to the venue and tell my fiancé. He is so disappointed. He tells me that I'm an awful and selfish person for lying to him and that he will never forgive me."

This approach can be useful in some cases, but when it comes to cases in which fear and doubt are central, I prefer to write scripts using uncertainty language. Such language includes words like could, can, might, and may. Since this word choice highlights uncertainty, these scripts really target the aim of ERP for those with fear-based obsessions. Folks don't have to accept that unwanted outcomes will definitely happen or that experiences will be as horrible as they fear. They just have to accept the *possibility* that bad things *could* happen and that they *might* be as devastating as predicted.

Using uncertainty language for OCD manifestations involving fear also helps prevent folks from mistakenly resigning themselves to upsetting possibilities as though they were foregone conclusions. No one knows the future, and so no one can definitively say whether something will or won't happen. Accepting the worst isn't the aim and using uncertainty language reduces the likelihood of unwittingly falling into resignation and depression.

If we were to reconfigure the above script using uncertainty language, it would sound like this:

"It's possible that on my wedding day I may wake up feeling anxious. I might try to brush it off, only to have the anxiety continuously build as I get dressed. It's possible that, on the drive to the venue, I could realize that my fiancé isn't the one and that I never should have agreed to marry him. I might decide to call off the wedding. I could hurt my fiancé deeply and he may never forgive me for selfishly waiting until the last minute to break the news."

Once you have written a script, you can record it and listen to it repeatedly, or you may choose to write it out and to read it repeatedly. This really is a matter of preference. The aim is to read or listen to the script regularly while refraining from trying to resolve the uncertainty and discomfort the script generates. As for the duration, we'll discuss that more in a bit.

Meanwhile, if some of your triggers aren't easily replicated, jot down some imaginal ideas, including words, phrases and possible stories, that could be triggering.

____

____

____

____

____

____

____

____

____

____

____

____

____

Remember: these triggers are meant to replicate obsessions so that we have the opportunity to practice response prevention. This means that after those triggers occur, we are tasked with disengaging from mental compulsions.

In Vivo Exposures

In vivo exposures will comprise the rest of your list. These are overt actions you can take to increase your distress. For someone with POCD, this might involve walking down the toy aisle or going to a store where children might be present.

If you avoid certain activities that are important to you—for instance, going to the grocery store—then doing in vivo exposures will be an important part of your recovery. If you tend to compulse following triggering activities, then you'll want to engage in these activities and refrain from compulsing. For example, if an attractive instructor at the gym triggers your sexual orientation obsessions, you might go to the gym and refrain from checking your feelings.

Getting out into the world and making a choice to trigger yourself is a scary prospect. Then again, so is the idea of perpetually avoiding things that matter to you because they might be triggering. There are lots of scary things in this life. The only thing we really get to choose is what kind of scary we prioritize.

Using the list of triggers you outlined earlier in the chapter, write down some different in vivo exposure ideas:

____

____

____

____

____

____

____

____

____

____

____

____

____

Duration, Frequency, and Application of Exposures

People often wonder if there's a specific recipe for doing exposures. How long should each individual exposure trial last? How often should exposures be repeated? When should you move on from working on a specific exposure altogether? Different schools of thought encourage different approaches.

Habituation

Traditional, habituation-based ERP instructed people to do an individual exposure trial until distress peaked and decreased substantially. When the trigger no longer provoked distress, they would cross the exposure off the hierarchy. As we've discussed, though, habituation isn't a strong indicator of long-term recovery and isn't a reliable metric. Besides, trying to habituate to every single trigger is often inefficient. We want you out living your life, not perpetually focused on therapeutic exercises.

Inhibitory Learning Theory

The formula for inhibitory learning is slightly different. With this approach, exposures are designed to promote learning. They often combine triggers and are done across contexts to help strengthen and generalize learning. So, someone with obsessions about throwing their child down a staircase might repeatedly listen to an imaginal script while holding their baby. They might also hold the baby at different second-story locations.

If this sounds scary, don't fret! Even within this model, you can start with a singular, less triggering exposure and take the process at your pace. While you may not be ready to take them on just yet, consider how you might combine different exposures on your hierarchy or practice exposures in different contexts:

____

____

____

____

Also, with inhibitory learning you'll consider your expectations about the outcome of doing the exposure before each exposure. Your expectations might directly involve the feared outcomes of your obsessions. For instance, someone with postpartum obsessions might expect that if they hold their baby for five minutes on a second story (exposure) then they will throw her down a staircase (expected response).

But as we've discussed throughout this book, fear isn't always central to OCD. Sometimes, folks do compulsions to avoid other emotions. Even when fear is central, the feared consequences of exposure may be so removed that it's not possible to directly test the expected outcome. For instance, holding a baby on the second story (exposure) wouldn't allow someone to test the expectation that, *someday* they might let their guard down and throw their baby down the stairs (expectation). The fear is too remote to directly assess.

If your fears are more remote or your obsessions involve other emotional experiences, you can consider your expectations regarding your capacity to tolerate distress. In the example, the postpartum OCD sufferer would consider their expectations for how they would cope while holding their baby on the second floor for five minutes (exposure). Perhaps they expect that they'll be unable to handle the anxiety about whether they will throw their baby down the stairs someday (expectation).

So, if the consequences you fear are more removed or you're not dealing with fear, consider: do you expect that the distress exposures cause will be too intense or that you will be unable to cope? Make note of the expected outcome. This will allow you to compare what you expect will happen with the actual outcome of the exposure:

____

____

____

____

Now consider how long you would need to do the exposure to test your expectations. If someone believed they could cope with holding the baby for one minute on the second story, then one minute wouldn't be long enough. If they didn't think they could handle five minutes, then they could do a five-minute exposure.

After the exposure, you'll reflect on the experience and consider:

1. Was your expectation accurate?

   In the example, we might ask, "Were you able to tolerate your fear?" Underscoring when your expectations are violated supports learning.

   ____

   ____

2. Are you surprised by the outcome? The element of surprise also facilitates learning.

   ____

   ____

In this model, you'd continue to do an exposure until you no longer expected the outcome you initially predicted. So, once the person with postpartum OCD believed they could handle the doubt associated with holding their baby on a second story for five minutes, then they would move on to another exposure.

You can incorporate elements of this approach as you build your hierarchy and start exposure work. It's very helpful to reflect on what we expect and what ultimately happens. Independent of exposures, there has yet to be an instance when you absolutely couldn't tolerate any emotion. You've legitimately managed to feel every single feeling you've had up until now. Recognizing the mismatch between our presumptions and reality can support our recovery.

Ultimately, though, our emphasis is on an ACT perspective of ERP. With ACT, the goal of ERP is to help people live meaningful lives. Thus, ERP practice is used as a form of training for accepting thoughts, feelings, urges, and sensations so that people can prioritize their values in the face of these internal experiences. Given this, it's important that people are able to verbalize how each item on their hierarchy serves what's meaningful to them. In the example above, a parent who values being present and supportive might hold their baby on the second story to increase their willingness to feel anxiety about taking the baby to doctor's appointments.

In the process of ERP from an ACT perspective, we want to gauge a person's degree of willingness to (1) do an exposure, (2) have obsessions, and (3) allow for doubt, anxiety, distress, discomfort, or any uncomfortable emotional experiences. The degree of distress an exposure causes is only indirectly relevant, as it can inform someone's willingness to do the exposure.

When the person is able to do the exposure without performing compulsions and is willing to continually engage in the exposure without doing compulsions, then the practice is no longer necessary as an exposure exercise, per se. The relapse prevention work is in continuing to live your life. In the example above, the parent would take the baby up a flight of stairs whenever life circumstances required.

Walking Through Your Hierarchy

Now that we have a list of exposures, we want to order them. More recent conceptualizations of treatment approach exposure hierarchies differently. Inhibitory learning theory, for instance, suggests that we don't need to address our exposures in a hierarchical fashion because we learn better when we are surprised by our own capacity.

While surprise is fantastic, we want to help you get your footing and to start with what you're willing to do. Given this, I typically rank anticipated distress levels for exposures and suggest people start with lower-level triggers. If you haven't been facing distressing experiences, you probably don't have a very strong belief in your own capacity, and sometimes starting with the smaller stuff helps us build our belief in our abilities. If someone is open to taking on a higher-level exposure given their values, then I wholeheartedly support them in doing so, keeping response prevention in mind.

While ACT hierarchies are typically ranked by willingness rather than distress, people often find it easier to rank how challenging they think an exposure will be. Besides, people are generally less willing to tolerate higher levels of distress. As a result, the rankings are often quite similar in practice. Also, since we don't necessarily go up the hierarchy in a specific order, there's plenty of flexibility to prioritize exposures based on your willingness to experience discomfort. Given this, we'll rank your exposures based on distress level with the understanding that you can hop around to different exposures if you're willing to tolerate the anticipated distress.

We will use what we call a SUDS, or subjective units of distress scale, to rank your anticipated distress. You can use a 0–10 scale, like the one depicted, so that you have a sense of how challenging you predict each exposure will be. In the ranking process, remember that you will be practicing response prevention because this will impact how much distress you anticipate.

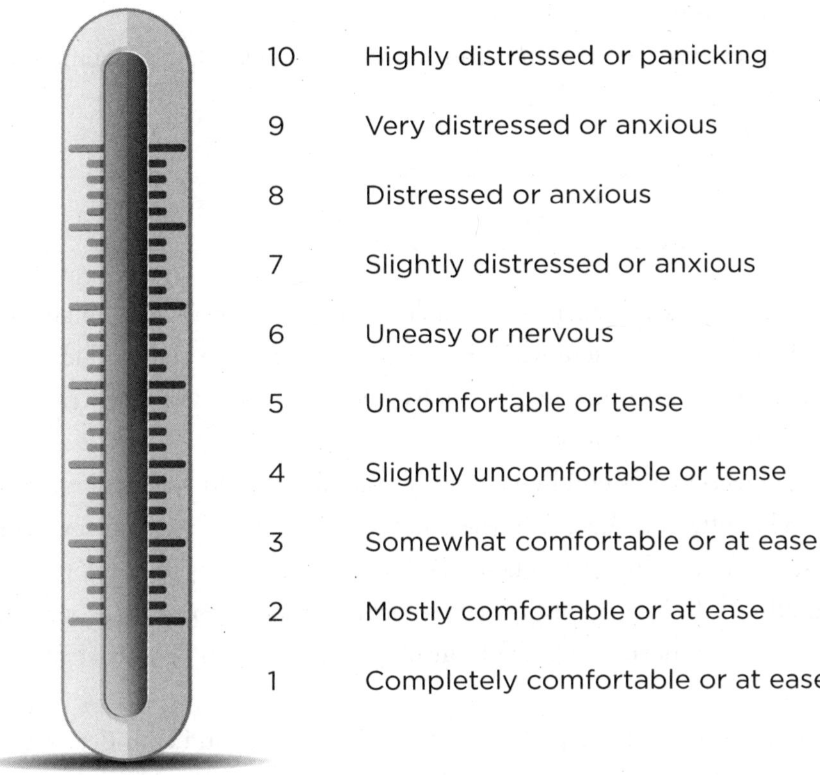

Once you've ordered them, you have a basic roadmap for facing your fears. But remember, exposures are only ever as good as their response prevention. You can face all the distressing triggers the world has to offer, but if you respond by trying to resolve uncertainty and discomfort, you are merely reinforcing the old, unhelpful pattern of relating to triggers. Exposure without response prevention—or at least response reduction—is triggering yourself on purpose and doing a compulsion. This is, akin to torturing yourself, and I wouldn't recommend it.

Ultimately, you may find some exposures are easier than you anticipate and others to be more challenging. This is not a problem. If an exposure is easier than you think it will be, you can move on to another. If it's more difficult, your ability to handle the difficulty will lead to surprise and support your learning.

Some exposures may not cause you distress, and this isn't a problem either! Again, it's your willingness to undertake exposures and feel whatever emotions arise during exposures that gives you the freedom to live life on your terms. And living life on your terms is the ultimate goal anyway, which takes us to one additional type of exposure.

Value-Driven Exposure and Response Prevention

Value-driven exposures add purpose to incidental and intentional exposures as they are expressly designed to get you closer to being the person that you want to be. Back in chapter 5, we discussed values from an ACT perspective, and you did an exercise to flesh out your values. These are the same values we will be drawing on in developing value-based exposures.

Copy your list of values in the space below so that you can reference them while developing related exposures.

____

____

How can values inform exposures? Let's consider an example. Someone with POCD might avoid spending time with their niece, which would interfere with their ability to prioritize their values in that relationship. For this person, a value-based exposure might involve spending time with their niece and expressing warmth by holding her while reading a story.

Of course, a person with POCD who avoids children might already have listed spending time with their niece as a form of exposure. The difference here is in the emphasis on *how* they show up with their niece. While this difference may seem minute, living a value-based life is a surefire way to develop pride in yourself. No matter what we're thinking or feeling, we always get to decide whether we prioritize our values. You can feel anxious and be kind. You can have thoughts of harming your niece and gently stroke their hair.

Now let's review the list of exposures we've developed throughout this chapter and consider how your values might influence these exposures. Can you tweak your exposures so that you're clearer about how they'll help you be the kind of person that you want to be?

____

____

____

____

____

____

Even if the exposures don't need to be tweaked, it's helpful to consider exactly how your exposures will help you be the kind of person you want to be. For those exposures that you don't adjust, consider how these exposures will help you get closer to those values you listed.

Keep in mind that response prevention is also informed by your values. If being present is important to you, then ruminating doesn't serve this purpose. If you value being generous, ruminating will make you more self-focused and ultimately self-centered.

While some values might be prioritized more in some settings than others, being the type of person you want to be usually transcends specific contexts. If kindness is a value of yours, then expressing kindness toward yourself, your best friend, or some random stranger are all part of expressing that value.

Consider below how your values might influence your choice to practice response prevention.

____

____

____

____

____

____

When avoidance and compulsions stand in the way of who you want to be, then your reasons for change are clear. Thus, values can help keep us motivated when the going gets tough. If you have anxiety about driving, you might be willing to drive to your friend's party to be supportive. If your friend triggers sexual-orientation obsessions, you might be willing to spend time with them to express care when they're struggling. Values give a whole lot of meaning to exposure work, making the benefits of exposure work more tangible.

Centering values can help with intrinsic motivation and, ultimately, with relapse prevention too. If we're clear on why we're practicing response prevention, and this why is directly related to our sense of meaning and purpose, we are less likely to find ourselves back down the rabbit hole of mental compulsions.

Values also empower us. When you prioritize avoiding distress or catastrophes at all costs, you'll constantly be looking over your shoulder as you run from thoughts and feelings. Living in this state of hypervigilance is distressing unto itself. If, instead, you focus on building something that matters to you, you'll be less focused on unwanted potential outcomes, more focused on what you can control, and more likely to recognize your own capacity in the process. Ultimately, values give you something to walk toward. Suddenly, you're on the offensive rather than perpetually playing defense. This is invigorating.

Beyond Recovery

You've made it! You and I are about to part ways, dear reader. You may wonder about the timing of this. Aren't we just beginning? Yes, in many ways this is just the beginning. Now you have a map for active exposure work, and it's time to start facing your triggers.

And you've also been doing the work already. You've learned practices to support you in disengaging from mental compulsions, and hopefully, you're already starting to see how meaningful it is to drop thinking in favor of living in the present. What's more, you know how your mind works. You can see your obsessions and mental compulsions more clearly. You've got a template for vetting thoughts and thinking more effectively. You know why you're facing your triggers, and you know how to accept your thoughts, feelings, and urges so you don't get stuck in the recesses of your mind. You have a better idea of how to be kind toward yourself. You know how to reorient your attention to what matters most to you and how to focus on cultivating your values.

So, you're not just starting. You're forging onward. And in some ways, we aren't parting, at all. You may recall that in the introduction, I suggested you use this book like a manual. As you go about the task of facing your triggers head-on, I hope you will reference the material throughout the book to support you in this undertaking. That's right—plot twist! This isn't actually the end because this book doesn't really have an end. All of the information is still available to you to return to in the event that you think a refresher would be helpful.

You may also remember that back at the beginning of the book I said recovery was within its pages, not at the end. And that's true. It's also true that recovery is beyond the pages of this book. I'm going to assume that you didn't start the recovery journey just to focus on distress all the time. Exposures, in general, are hugely important. But, once you're willing to take on any exposure, and you've given yourself the opportunity to deliberately practice response prevention with intentional exposures, living becomes the priority.

As such, our end goal is to focus primarily on values-based living more broadly. This will undoubtedly include plenty of value-based exposures and will require us to navigate what incidental exposures come up on the journey. Fortunately, if you're committed to moving toward what matters to you, you're less likely to get chased off course by uncomfortable emotions.

Beyond OCD, your values can help you build lasting contentment. When you reflect on your day and recognize you did your utmost to be the person that you want to be, you will have a sense of fulfillment independent of experiences that are beyond your control. This is so much bigger than OCD recovery. This is about you building a life you can be proud of.

Centering what matters most to you is the basis for a life well-lived. I know that you probably picked up this book to stop your OCD-related suffering. And hey, don't get me wrong, reducing suffering is great! But nothing really compares to building a life that is meaningful to you. My hope is that in guiding you toward your values, this book can help you access something greater than reduced suffering. Maybe, just maybe, this book can help you live life in a way you wouldn't have thought to if you'd never struggled with OCD.

Maybe the support you've gained as a result of the problem you wished you'd never had can help you live a bigger more beautiful life than you otherwise would have.

As we draw this chapter and book to a close, this is my hope for you. May your life be rich, meaningful, and fulfilling. May you never let thoughts or feelings alone stand in the way of what matters to you. May you appreciate your own capacity to live a bold life on your terms.

References

Beck, J. S. 2011. *Cognitive Behavior Therapy: Basics and Beyond.* 2nd ed. NY: Guilford Publications.

Bouvard, M., N. Fournet, A. Denis, A. Sixdenier, and D. Clark. 2017. "Intrusive Thoughts in Patients with Obsessive Compulsive Disorder and Non-Clinical Participants: A Comparison Using the International Intrusive Thought Interview Schedule. *Cognitive Behaviour Therapy* 46(4):287–299. https://doi.org/10.1080/16506073.2016.1262894

Chien, W.T., M. Tse, H.Y. Chan, H.Y. Cheng, and L. Chen. 2022. "Is Mindfulness-Based Intervention an Effective Treatment for People with Obsessive-Compulsive Disorder? A Systematic Review and Meta-Analysis." *Journal of Obsessive-Compulsive and Related Disorders. 32*:1–11. https://doi.org/10.1016/j.jocrd.2022.100712

Clark, R. E. 2004. The Classical Origins of Pavlov's Conditioning. *Integrative Physiological and Behavioral Science: The Official Journal of the Pavlovian Society* 39(4):279–294. https://doi.org/10.1007/BF02734167

Covey, S. R., A. R. Merrill, and R. R. Merrill. 1996. *First Things First.* NY: Free Press.

Craske, M. G., M. Treanor, C.C. Conway, T. Zbozinek, and B. Vervliet. 2014. Maximizing Exposure Therapy: An Inhibitory Learning Approach. *Behaviour Research and Therapy* 58:10–23. https://doi.org/10.1016/j.brat.2014.04.006

Ekman, P. 1992. "Are There Basic Emotions?" *Psychological Review* 99(3):550–553. https://doi.org/10.1037/0033-295X.99.3.550

Ferrando, C. and C. Selai. 2021. A Systematic Review and Meta-Analysis on the Effectiveness of Exposure and Response Prevention Therapy in the Treatment of Obsessive-Compulsive Disorder. *Journal of Obsessive-Compulsive and Related Disorders* 31: 100684. https://doi.org/10.1016/j.jocrd.2021.100684

Ferrão, J. V. B., M.C. do Rosário, L.F. Fontenelle, and Y.A. Ferrão. 2023. "Prevalence and Psychopathology Features of Mental Rituals in Patients with Obsessive-Compulsive Disorder: A Descriptive Exploratory Study of 1001 Patients." *Clinical Psychology & Psychotherapy* 30(6):1520–1533. https://doi.org/10.1002/cpp.2890

Harris, R. 2008. *The Happiness Trap: How to Stop Struggling and Start Living.* NY: Random House.

Harris, R. 2021. *Trauma-Focused ACT: A Practitioner's Guide to Working with Mind, Body and Emotions Using Acceptance and Commitment Therapy.* CA: Context Press

Hershfield, J. 2015. *When a Family Member Has OCD: Mindfulness and Cognitive Behavioral Skills to Help Families Affected by Obsessive-Compulsive Disorder.* CA: New Harbinger Publications.

IOCDF. 2014. *How to Find the Right Therapist*. Retrieved April 27, 2025 from https://iocdf.org/ocd-finding-help/how-to-find-the-right-therapist/

Jacoby, R. J., and J.S. Abramowitz. 2016. "Inhibitory Learning Approaches to Exposure Therapy: A Critical Review and Translation to Obsessive-Compulsive Disorder. *Clinical Psychology Review* 49:28–40. https://doi.org/10.1016/j.cpr.2016.07.001

Joubert, A. E., A.B. Grierson, I. Li, M.J. Sharrock, M.L. Moulds, A. Werner-Seidler, E.P. Stech, A.E.J. Mahoney, and J.M. Newby. 2023. "Managing Rumination and Worry: A Randomised Controlled Trial of an Internet Intervention Targeting Repetitive Negative Thinking Delivered With and Without Clinician Guidance. *Behaviour Research and Therapy* 168: 104378. https://doi.org/10.1016/j.brat.2023.104378

Kabat-Zinn, J. 2023. *Wherever You Go, There You Are: Mindfulness Meditation in Everyday Life.* NY: Balance.

Lenzen, M. "Feeling Our Emotions." *Scientific American*, April 2005. https://www.scientificamerican.com/article/feeling-our-emotions/

Li, Y., and C. Tang. 2024. "A Systematic Review of the Effects of Rumination-Focused Cognitive Behavioral Therapy in Reducing Depressive Symptoms. *Frontiers in Psychology*, 15: 1447207. https://doi.org/10.3389/fpsyg.2024.1447207

Neff, K. and C. Germer. 2018. *The Mindful Self-Compassion Workbook: A Proven Way to Accept Yourself, Build Inner Strength, and Thrive.* NY: Guilford Press.

Pal, V., S. Ramdurg, and S. Chaukimath. 2024. "Assessment of the Prevalence and Types of Mental Compulsions in Patients With Obsessive-Compulsive Disorder in North Karnataka: A Cross-Sectional Study." *Cureus* 16(10): e71960. https://doi.org/10.7759/cureus.71960

Reid, J. E., K.R. Laws, L. Drummond, M. Vismara, B. Grancini, D. Mpavaenda, and N.A. Fineberg. 2021. "Cognitive Behavioural Therapy with Exposure and Response Prevention in the Treatment of Obsessive-Compulsive Disorder: A Systematic Review and Meta-Analysis of Randomised Controlled Trials. *Comprehensive Psychiatry* 106: 152223. https://doi.org/10.1016/j.comppsych.2021.152223

Riquelme-Marín, A., A.I. Rosa-Alcázar, and J.M. Ortigosa-Quiles. "Mindfulness-Based Psychotherapy in Patients with Obsessive-Compulsive Disorder: A Meta-Analytical Study." *International Journal of Clinical and Health Psychology* 22(3): 100321. https://doi.org/10.1016/j.ijchp.2022.100321

Rosa-Alcázar, A. I., J. Sánchez-Meca, A. Gómez-Conesa, and F. Marín-Martínez. 2008. "Psychological Treatment of Obsessive-Compulsive Disorder: A Meta-Analysis. *Clinical Psychology Review* 28(8):1310–1325. https://doi.org/10.1016/j.cpr.2008.07.001Shantideva. 2022. *Bodhisattvacaryāvatāra: Entering the Way of the Bodhisattvas.* Translated by Khenpo Gawang Rinpoche and Gerry Weiner. Duhuang Edition. Memphis, TN: Jeweled Lotus Publications.

Shavitt, R. G., M.A. de Mathis, F. Oki, Y.A. Ferrao, L.R. Fontenelle, A.R. Torres, J.B. Diniz, D.L. Costa, M.C. do Rosário, M.Q. Hoexter, E.C. Miguel, and H.B. Simpson. 2014. "Phenomenology of OCD: Lessons from a Large Multicenter Study and Implications for ICD-11. *Journal of Psychiatric Research* 57:141–148. https://doi.org/10.1016/j.jpsychires.2014.06.010

Sibrava, N. J., C.L. Boisseau, M.C. Mancebo, J.L. Eisen, and S.A. Rasmussen. 2011. "Prevalence and Clinical Characteristics of Mental Rituals in a Longitudinal Clinical Sample of Obsessive-Compulsive Disorder. *Depression and Anxiety* 28(10):892–898. https://doi.org/10.1002/da.20869

Skinner, B. F. 1976. *Operant Conditioning.* NY: Vintage.

Soondrum, T., X. Wang, F. Gao, Q. Liu, J. Fan, and X. Zhu. 2022. "The Applicability of Acceptance and Commitment Therapy for Obsessive-Compulsive Disorder: A Systematic Review and Meta-Analysis." *Brain Sciences* 12(5): 656. https://doi.org/10.3390/brainsci12050656

Taylor, J. B. 2008. *My Stroke of Insight: A Brain Scientist's Personal Journey.* NY: Penguin Books.

Tseng, J., and J. Poppenk. 2020. Brain Meta-State Transitions Demarcate Thoughts Across Task Contexts Exposing the Mental Noise of Trait Neuroticism. *Nature Communications* 11(1): 3480. https://doi.org/10.1038/s41467-020-17255-9

Tulbure, B. T., D.P. Dudau, S. Marian, and E. Watkins. 2025. "An Internet-Delivered Rumination-Focused CBT Intervention for Adults with Depression and Anxiety: A Randomized Controlled Trial." *Behavior Therapy* 56(1). https://doi.org/10.1016/j.beth.2024.12.004

Twohig, M. P., J.S. Abramowitz, E.J. Bluett, L.E. Fabricant, R.J. Jacoby, K.L. Morrison, L. Reuman, and B.M. Smith. 2015. "Exposure Therapy for OCD from an Acceptance and Commitment Therapy (ACT) Framework. *Journal of Obsessive-Compulsive and Related Disorders* 6:167–173. https://doi.org/10.1016/j.jocrd.2014.12.007

Twohig, M. P., L.K. Capel, and M.E. Levin. 2024. A Review of Research on Acceptance and Commitment Therapy for Anxiety and Obsessive-Compulsive and Related Disorders. *The Psychiatric Clinics of North America* 47(4):711–722. https://doi.org/10.1016/j.psc.2024.04.013

Van Noppen, B., S. Sassano-Higgins, R. Appasani, and F. Sapp. 2021. Cognitive-Behavioral Therapy for Obsessive-Compulsive Disorder: 2021 Update. *Focus (American Psychiatric Publishing)* 19(4):430–443. https://doi.org/10.1176/appi.focus.20210015

Watkins, E. R., E. Mullan, J. Wingrove, K. Rimes, H. Steiner, N. Bathurst, R. Eastman, J. Scott. 2011. Rumination-Focused Cognitive–Behavioural Therapy for Residual Depression: Phase II Randomised Controlled Trial. *British Journal of Psychiatry* 199:317–322. https://doi.org/10.1192/bjp.bp.110.090282

Watkins, E. R. 2016. *Rumination-Focused Cognitive-Behavioral Therapy for Depression.* NY: Guilford Press.

Lauren Rosen, LMFT, has dedicated her career to providing compassionate, evidence-based psychotherapy to those with obsessive-compulsive disorder (OCD) and anxiety disorders. She graduated summa cum laude from UCLA with her BA in psychology, earned her master's in clinical psychology from Antioch University, and trained at the OCD Center of Los Angeles. In 2022, Lauren founded the Center for the Obsessive Mind, an outpatient clinic serving individuals in California, Florida, Utah, Nevada, Oregon, Pennsylvania, and select other states and countries. She and her team use exposure and response prevention (ERP), acceptance and commitment therapy (ACT), and mindfulness-based cognitive behavioral therapy (MBCBT), to help people take their lives back from anxiety, distress, and intrusive thoughts. Lauren is author of *The Mental Compulsions Workbook for OCD*. You can find Lauren on Instagram and via the *Purely OCD Podcast*.

Foreword writer **Kimberley Quinlan, LMFT**, is a psychotherapist in private practice specializing in the treatment of OCD and related disorders. She is host of the *Your Anxiety Toolkit* podcast, and founder of www.cbtschool.com—an online psychoeducation platform for OCD, anxiety disorders, and body-focused repetitive behaviors (BFRBs).